M000308629

GET THAT PROJECT MANAGEMENT JOB!

Master the Job Interview and get hired

George T. Edwards

Get That Project Management Job! - Master the Job Interview and get hired

By George T. Edwards
Blue Crystal Press
Atlanta, GA

Copyright © 2007 by George T. Edwards
All rights reserved
Cover background image is Licensed Material from Getty Images
All other images are copyright © 2000-2007 by George T. Edwards

Cover Design:
Blue Crystal Press

Notice of Rights

No part of this book may be reproduced or transmitted in any form or by any means, electronic or mechanical, including photocopying, recording, or by any information storage and retrieval system, without the prior written permission of the Publisher.

Notice of Liability

The information given in this book is written in good faith. Even as the content of this book has been researched, some portions could be considered speculative in its own nature. Therefore, the information should be used responsibly and at your own discretion. The information in this book is distributed on an "as is" basis, without warranty. Neither the author, the publisher nor the companies owned by the author shall have any liability to any person or entity with respect to any loss or damage caused by or alleged to be caused directly or indirectly by the information contained in this book.

This publication is designed to provide accurate and authoritative information in regard to the subject matter covered. It is sold with the understanding that the publisher is not engaged in providing professional service.

Trademarks

Blue Crystal Press, Get That Project Management Job! - Master the Job Interview and get hired

Blue Crystal Press
Atlanta, GA
Find us on the World Wide Web www.bluecrystalpress.com
We want to hear from you. Please send comments, suggestions and concerns to readers@bluecrystalpress.com

George T. Edwards

Table of Contents

Introduction – Job Interviews in the Marketplace   8

How to Use this Book   8

Part 1 – Job Interview Questions and Answers   **10**

Section 1   The Job Interview   **10**
Preparation is Key   10
Interview Basics   10
The Interview is a Sale   11
Behavioral Interviews   12
The STAR Method   14
Case questions   14
Skills   15
Finding out What They Need   15
Being Yourself?   16
General Advice   16
Body Language   17
Before the Interview   18
During the Interview   18
Questions to Ask the Job Interviewer   19
Closing the Interview in a Great Way   19
Questions and Answers   20
Preparation for the Job Interview – One More Time   21

Section 2   Generic Interview Q & A   **21**
2.1   Tell me about yourself   21
2.2   Why did you leave XYZ Company?   23
2.3   Which of your jobs did you like best? Why?   23
2.4   How did you get your past jobs?   24
2.5   Why are you so interested in our company?   24
2.6   Why are you so interested in this particular job?   25
2.7   What are your long-range and short-range plans?   25
2.8   If you had complete freedom, what job would you choose?   26
2.9   What are your top strengths?   26
2.10   What are your weaknesses?   27

Section 3   Project Management Interview Q & A   **28**
3.1   Can you tell me about a problem you encountered while managing a
        project and how you dealt with it?   28
3.2   How do you handle disruptive team members?   29
3.3   How do you handle non-productive team members?   31

3.4	How do you motivate team members who are burned out or bored?	32
3.5	How do you motivate people?	33
3.6	How do you handle team members who come to you with their personal problems?	34
3.7	Explain how you operate interdepartmentally.	35
3.8	Tell me how you would react to a situation where there was more than one way to accomplish the same task, and there were very strong feelings by others on each position.	35
3.9	What is your management style?	35
3.10	What do you look for when you hire people?	36
3.11	Give me an example of your leadership involvement where teamwork played an important role.	37
3.12	How do you start a project?	37
3.13	What are the basic components of a project plan?	38
3.14	If you are teaching the ropes to a new Project Manager, what would you say are the most important things he needs to look for?	38
3.15	What would be the key artifacts needed in a project?	39
3.16	How do you manage change?	39
3.17	How do you manage conflict in the project team?	40
3.18	How do you deal with a difficult team member?	41
3.19	What qualifications are required to be an effective project manager?	42
3.20	Your three-month project is about to exceed the projected budget after the first month. What steps will you take to address the potential cost overrun?	43
3.21	You are given the assignment of project manager and the team members have already been identified. To increase the effectiveness of your project team, what steps will you take?	43
3.22	You have been assigned as the project manager for a team comprised of new employees just out of college and "entry-level" consulting staff. What steps can you take to insure that the project is completed against a very tight time deadline?	44
3.23	What is the difference between a project plan and a project schedule? What do you include in a project schedule?	44
3.24	How do you track a project?	44
3.25	How do you track risks? Tell me about the risks that your last project had.	45
3.26	What is the difference between a risk and an issue?	46
3.27	How do you define quality in project management?	46
3.28	What is the difference between quality management and quality control?	47
3.29	At what time in the project do you start quality control?	47
3.30	What would you say if a team member asks why project management is needed? Why do we have to do all this documentation ahead of the real work?	48
3.31	What have you learned in obtaining your PMP that you are using in real-life projects?	49
3.32	How do you make sure that outside companies meet their deadlines?	49
3.33	What do you do if a team member presents a work product that you know	

	for a fact is flawed or incomplete, but the team member insists it is completed and sound?	50
3.34	What would you do if a manager whose resources you are using keeps saying that all the documentation required by the project is getting in the way of actual progress?	51
3.35	What was the CMM level at your current/last job?	52
3.36	Describe what you did in a difficult project environment to get the job done on time and on budget.	52
3.37	What was the biggest problem you faced on your last project? And how did you address it?	53
3.38	What was your role in your last project?	53
3.39	What was the most interesting role you played in a project?	54
3.40	What is the most common reason why projects fail?	54
3.41	What do you do when a team member does not complete his/her assignment and has gone to another project?	54
3.42	Have you used Microsoft Project? How do you like it?	54
3.43	How do you verify that the requirements identified for a project are actually included in the final delivery to the users?	55
3.44	Are you detail-oriented or big-picture-oriented?	55
3.45	Would you call yourself tough-minded and thick-skinned?	55
3.46	What are your greatest strengths and weaknesses in the Project Management areas of knowledge?	55
3.47	What are the risks you had in your last project?	56
3.48	What is the role of Information Technology in a company	56
3.49	Name three signs that indicate your project may fail.	56
3.50	More Questions	56

Section 4	**Job Interviewer Guide**	**61**
	How to Interview	61
	Can They Do the Job?	62
	How Well do They Function Under Pressure?	62
	How Will They Fit In?	63

Part 2	**Project Management Theory**	**65**

Section 1	**Project Management in One Page (or Three)**	**65**
	Define the Scope and Objectives	65
	Define the Deliverables	65
	Project Planning	65
	Communication	66
	Tracking and Reporting Project Progress	66
	Change Management	66
	Risk Management	67

Section 2	**Project Management and its Context**	**68**
2.1	Project Management	68

2.2   The Traditional Triple Constraint   69

2.3   Project Stakeholders   70
2.4   Attributes of a Project Manager   70
2.5   Project Life Cycle   70
2.6   Project Phases   72
2.7   Projects and Organizations   74
2.8   Functional Organization   75
2.9   Projectized Organization   76
2.10   Matrix Organization   76
2.11   Project Management Office   79

Section 3   Project Management Areas of Knowledge   80

Section 4   Project Integration Management   81
4.1   Project Plan Development   81
4.2   Project Plan Execution   82
4.3   Change Control   82

Section 5   Project Scope Management   82
5.1   Scope Initiation   82
5.2   Scope Definition   85
5.3   Scope Change Control   86
5.4   Scope Verification   87

Section 6   Project Time Management   87
6.1   Network Diagrams   88
6.2   Gantt Chart   88
6.3   Calculating the Project Duration   89
6.4   Critical Path Method   89
6.5   PERT – Program Evaluation and Review Technique   90
6.6   Project Schedule Control   90
6.7   Earned Value   91

Section 7   Project Cost Management   93
7.1   Resource Planning   93
7.2   Cost Estimating   94
7.3   Cost Control   95

Section 8   Project Quality Management   95
8.1   Quality of the Project Management Process   96
8.2   Quality Assurance   96
8.3   Six Sigma   97
8.4   Quality Management Process   98
8.5   Other Key Quality Concepts   98

Section 9   Project Human Resource Management   99
9.1   Project Team Management   99
9.2   Motivation Theories   100
9.3   Management Styles   101

Section 10   Project Communications Management   102
10.1   Communications Planning   102
10.2   Information Distribution   103
10.3   Performance Reporting   103
10.4   Administrative Closure   104
10.5   Suggestions for Improving Project Communications   104
10.6   Conflict Handling Modes   104
10.7   Running Effective Meetings   104

Section 11   Project Risk Management   105
11.1   Risk Management   105
11.2   Risk Management Process   106
11.3   Risk Management Plan   106
11.4   Risk Identification Tools   107
11.5   Qualitative Risk Analysis   107
11.6   Quantitative Risk Analysis   107
11.7   Risk Response Planning   108
11.8   Other Risk Definitions   109

Section 12   Procurement Management   109
12.1   Requirements for a Contract   109
12.2   Solicitation Tools   109
12.3   Contract Administration   110
12.4   Contract Types   110

About the Author   112

Introduction

Job Interviews in the Marketplace

Just like in most work places, the interesting projects and the promotions do not necessarily go to those most qualified, the hiring process and the job interview as they are conducted today in too many job sites do not necessarily end with the hiring of the most qualified person but of the one that presents itself better. This book will help you excel at the job interview to maximize your chances of being hired.

During a job interview, candidates are subject to tremendous stress. They are judged on what they say and how they say it. The job seeker has to answer specific questions and must also display knowledge, experience and sought-after character traits. In addition, he/she should be gathering information about the job and the company. The candidate who performs the best in this complex situation usually gets the job.

It is important to understand that a resume, a PMP certification, a degree, networking or other means can get you an interview, but only excelling at the job interview will get you the job. It is during the job interview that you must prove that you can actually do the job and that you want to do it. If you perform badly in the interview, no matter how good your resume looks or how good your references are, it is most likely that you will not get the job.

The job interview is the critical gateway to a new position, and a job seeker cannot be prepared enough for it. This book will give you the questions that are most likely to be asked, the understanding of why they are asked and how to avoid mistakes. You will be prepared for the interview process and will understand the concept behind behavioral interviews. Most importantly, it will give you the right answers to all those frequently asked questions so that you will excel in the interview, quickly getting the job offer. In short, this book will help you perform in a stellar way.

How to Use this Book

The purpose of this book is to help you land the job and for that we created two complementary parts. The first part covers the interview in general, the basic strategies you should follow, general behavioral questions that you should master and the questions most frequently asked in a project management job interview with suggested answers. The second part is all about project management theory and will help refresh project management questions for the technical interviews you may have.

The questions discussed in this book are actually used in job interviews and have been posed to the author or to people who have been interviewed for this book. Also included are questions the author has asked when interviewing job candidates. Additional questions found in related literature as well as questions that have stumped job candidates and have been posed on our website have been included.

Some questions include comments about the reasoning behind the question, because certain questions are used in more than one way to elicit information from the candidate.

A single incorrect answer can rule you out, but a couple of right answers can put you at the top of the list. This book will give you packed answers that will give you that edge. Knowing the right answer is good, but it is equally as important to know what the wrong answer is. There are several instances in this book where wrong answers are discussed.

The answers in this book address the specific questions that are going to be asked and have been prepared to deliver information that you want the interviewer to know and that will present your experience and skills in the best light.

By knowing in advance how to answer most of the questions that will be asked, you will have the confidence you need to turn the interview into your best weapon. By showing more knowledge, more experience and more confidence, you will not only be offered the job, but you may receive a higher offer.

Finding a job is stressful, especially if one is not currently working. There is a need to prepare for the job hunt quickly, and this book gives you the advice you need in a summary format. It is concise, informative and to the point.

You'd better know the answers – there is no second chance.

Part 1 - Job Interview Questions and Answers

Section 1   The Job Interview

Interviewing provides you with an opportunity to showcase your experience, knowledge, skills and aspirations to make you a desirable candidate for a given position and organization. The interview setting also allows you to demonstrate your interpersonal skills, professionalism and personal style. While most people claim (in resumes and cover letters) to possess interpersonal or communication skills, interviews provide you with the opportunity to demonstrate your skills.

Remember the goal: The interviewer is trying to determine three things:

1. Can you do the job? Do you have the experience, skill and what it takes to do the job?
2. Will you do the job? Would the job keep you interested and would you keep the job?
3. Will you fit in the company?

Your answers must address those three questions to the satisfaction of the interviewer.

Preparation is Key

By anticipating the questions, you can think through and practice your responses in advance and go into the interview with confidence. Minimize nervousness by practicing your responses, mentally clarifying your qualifications for the position and realizing that an interview is a mutual exchange of information between two interested parties. In short, minimize uncertainties and be ready for unexpected twists and turns presented by the interviewer.

The best way to prepare for the interview is to have answers prepared and stories ready to relay, but those stories must be linked to the job, to the job requirements, to the skill sought, to the position, the company or the industry.

Interview Basics

> ➤ Be prepared
> ➤ Make it a conversation
> ➤ Keep your answers brief
> ➤ Listen carefully
> ➤ Make connections for the interviewer

➢ Don't be modest and don't exaggerate
➢ Never present a strong personal view
➢ Never argue or defend a view during the interview

The Interview is a Sale

Look at interviewing as a sales process. In this process, you are both the product and the salesperson. The interview is your opportunity to "sell" the prospective employer on the benefits you can bring to the organization.

The best approach to making the sale is to find out what the "buyer's" needs are and communicating and demonstrating how you can satisfy those needs. In order to find the buyer's needs, you must research the organization before the actual interview. Find their website and review their financial results, press releases and their ads for other positions. The job ads are an excellent source of information about the company organization.

The heart of any successful interview, therefore, is asking appropriate questions to discover what kinds of problems the "buyer" (who has the open position) is having, and what the implications of those problems are. Then you begin to "sell" the benefits of your employment.

The best way to know exactly what the company is looking for is to ask questions during the interview. How to ask those questions is described later in this book. Once you know what the company's needs are, you must sell them on the benefits that you bring to the table to address those needs.

In a job search, the features are your skills, knowledge, degrees, certifications and experience. Describing the features is part of the sales process but the *benefits* are going to make the sale. The benefits are your accomplishments, the results you have been able to produce (productivity, profitability), and the solutions you can provide.

During the interview you must talk about the results of your work and achievements, not about the positions you held. When answering questions in a job interview, you must talk about the benefits you bring as opposed to the features. The fact that you have a PMP certification, or that you have taken project management classes may have helped you get the interview, but during the interview you must talk about what you accomplished with the knowledge you acquired and what you can do for the company.

You must keep in mind that the interview is a conversation in which the employer has a need that you are going to fulfill. They need somebody to do the work, and their need is as important as your need for a job. They need to find the right candidate, and you need to find the right job.

The employer, too, is under pressure to fill the position with a quality individual and may be anxious to find someone immediately. The interviewer has hopes and concerns just as you do. Think of an interview as a professional conversation between two parties who each have needs the other might satisfy.

This book will help you sell yourself as the best candidate so you can concentrate on finding the right job for you.

Behavioral Interviews

More and more companies are currently doing behavioral interviews. While interviews with hiring managers or peers might not be behavioral, the interviews with human resources most likely will be.

Behavioral interviewing is based on the premise that past behavior is the best predictor of future behavior, and it focuses on what candidates have done in the past, not on what they say they might do in the future. This allows hiring managers to assess applicants/candidates more fairly and objectively than other methods.

Behavior-based questions require you to provide specific examples concerning what you have done in the past. Behavioral interview questions usually begin with:

- Give an example of a time in which you ...
- Tell me about a time when circumstances required you to ...
- Describe the most significant ...
- Recall the most ...

Interviewers pose structured, open-ended questions to determine which skills candidates have used successfully in prior positions. Knowing how the applicant acted can help employers to more confidently predict how well the candidate might perform in a particular job.

Before a behavioral interview, hiring managers and human resources professionals identify specific competencies needed to succeed in the position, including technical and performance skills. From these competencies, the interviewers develop a list of questions that are designed to elicit descriptions of skills candidates have used in the past. Ideally, each candidate is asked the same questions in order to ensure uniformity. This process allows candidates to be judged on what they've done, not on their personalities. Later in this book you will find several behavioral questions that assess specific skills and competencies sought in for the position of project manager.

To succeed in a behavioral interview you must be able to relate stories that link your experience and skills to:

- The position
- The key competencies the employer wants
- The company and the company culture

Don't wait for the interview to think about these stories. You should have them ready ahead of time. For positive job stories about the position, reread the job description and come up with two or three specific examples of things you have done well that relate to the responsibilities of the job. You will use these stories during the job interview, even if not asked directly, by finding an opening that will permit you to launch into success stories that link to the key competencies the company is seeking.

Finally, for background on the company and the company culture, research the company thoroughly through their website. Review their financial results, press releases and ads for other positions. The job ads can be an excellent source of information about the company and its culture.

Sample of behavior-based questions:

- ➤ Describe a situation where you wish you had acted differently with someone at work. What did you do? What happened as a result?
- ➤ What are some of the most difficult one-to-one meetings you have had with subordinates? Why were they difficult?
- ➤ Describe an experience you had in which you were too persistent. What happened?
- ➤ Tell me about a time when you consulted your superior before taking action.
- ➤ Give me an example of a time when your ideas were strongly opposed in a discussion with superiors. How did you react? What were the results?
- ➤ How did your project management style, in terms of strengths and weaknesses, differ from the style used by others in the same job?
- ➤ Give me an example of a time when you had responsibility for the successful outcome of a very large project.
- ➤ Tell me about a time you had a major conflict with a colleague. How did you approach problem resolution?
- ➤ Why did you leave your job at the *ABC Company*?
- ➤ Describe a time when you were working under pressure and had to go the extra mile.
- ➤ What would your last supervisor say are your three best qualities? Why?

- ➢ What would your direct reports say?
- ➢ Given the list of job objectives, which are you happiest to see? In what order?
- ➢ Of all your projects, which was the most satisfying/least rewarding?

The STAR Method

The STAR approach is the way to answer behavioral questions. STAR stands for Situation or Task, Action, Results.

Situation or Task
Describe the situation you were in or the task that you needed to accomplish. It must be a specific event or situation, and not a generalized description of what you have done in the past. Be sure to give enough detail for the interviewer to understand. This situation can be from a previous job, from a volunteer experience or any relevant event. The closer the example is to a real everyday work situation, the better the example will be.

Action
Describe the action you took, and be sure to keep the focus on you. Even if you are discussing a group project or effort, describe what you did -- not the efforts of the team. Don't tell what you might do; tell what you did.

Result:
Describe what happened. What was accomplished?

It is very difficult to do all this if you have not prepared yourself. You will find solid examples of answers later in this book where we answer the most frequently asked questions.

Case questions

Some interviewers may ask you to solve a problem or pose a question that forces you think . (How many meetings are held in a 12 month project with 20 people?)
Case interview questions are meant to be very vague at the outset. The hiring manager is judging your ability to approach the problem in a methodical manner by asking the right questions in the right sequence so you can frame your answer. It is not the final answer what they are looking for but how you approach the problem.

Skills

Project management job descriptions vary greatly from industry to industry and even from company to company in the same industry, but the basic skills that companies are looking for in a project manager are:

- Communication skills
- Organizational skills
- Attention to detail
- Ability to work in a team environment
- Ability to effectively matrix manage within the organization
- Ability to multi-task
- Persistency
- Conflict management and conflict resolution
- Ability to work in an ambiguous environment
- Ability to influence and persuade
- Ability to work with a diverse team
- Strong customer service orientation
- Ability to bridge technical and non-technical resources

You must have a story relating to your past work which shows that you used those skills. You will see examples in the Questions and Answers section.

Find Out What They Need

A successful job hunter will not only answer questions in a winning way, but will also ask questions to find out exactly what the company needs. Let them start with a couple of questions before you ask one of your own. The Question and Answer section has some pertinent questions to ask, but in general you can take the question you receive and ask related questions back to the interviewer. For instance, if they ask, "Do you have a PMP certification?" Answer their inquiry and then ask questions such as "Are people here encouraged to get the certifications? Are most people working on their certifications?"

You must not be as inquisitive as they are, and you must be prepared to back off, but you can get more information by following up with a question that explores why they are asking you that particular question. So you could ask, "Why is a PMP certification valued by your company?"

Being Yourself?

A piece of advice that is often given when taking psychology tests and in interviews is to be one's self, but I think this is bad advice. Most people exhibit some modified behavior at work. For instance, a boxer might be naturally aggressive and not inclined to resolve issues by communicating and using teamwork (think Mike Tyson). However, the boxer must adapt his natural behavior if he wants to succeed in business. His job is not only boxing, but also managing himself in order to make money. To manage himself, he has to modify his behavior when doing business. Most people must adapt their natural behavior to succeed in the job environment and accept some situations that the natural self would dislike.

One example of adaptation involves corporate politics. The truth is that most people would rather not deal with office politics, but they realize that if they don't apply themselves to it, they will lose the good projects and may lose the job when times are tough. Some project managers land a role by being good programmers and being good analysts, but they must adapt to teamwork and to getting things done by influencing, which in many circumstances is not their natural behavior pattern.

Just being one's self is not the way to succeed at work. On the contrary, one must modify his or her behavior to meet job conditions, job requirements and the realities of society. For the same reasons, one should not just be one's self during the interview. You must be the person you are willing to be in the job you are applying for. If you are not willing to adapt to keep and succeed at a job, don't apply for it.

Can the interviewers see through the fact that you are not exactly being yourself? It depends how far you are stretching. If you have worked as a heads-down programmer for several years and are very good at what you do, you might be introverted and prefer to work by yourself, so it will be difficult for you to exhibit the exuberance of salespersons.

To succeed at your work, you must really enjoy it. If you have to adapt your behavior to the point that it becomes a job in itself, you probably will not succeed in that job.

General advice

Practice aloud for your interview. It will help you sound more polished and concise, and you will be less nervous in the actual interview.

List a few key things you want the employer to know about you, and review common interview questions. Formulate answers to those questions and answer them aloud while looking at yourself in the mirror. This exercise will prevent you from rambling, sounding unpolished or unsure during the interview. It will also help you discover what really does make you the best candidate for the job!

Name-dropping in an interview is a good way to make connections. You should use the names of companies you have worked for directly or indirectly and also refer to books you have read that are widely known in the industry (*PMBOK*, *One-Minute Manager*, *In Search of Excellence*). As an example, you can say, "I do *XYZ*, which I learned from reading *The One-Minute Manager* and have adapted it to my work." Don't hesitate to quote popular sayings such as, "I do believe that 'you must plan the work and work the plan' ", or "I follow the time-tested saying 'fail to plan is plan to fail'."

If you are going to talk about a specific company, be sure you know the names of the chief executives. If you are interviewing with a professional recruiter, they may know the names of the top people in the company you mention, so it is important that you know those names.

Don't hesitate to talk fondly of a prior boss. Your potential bosses will be delighted to hear that you had great respect for your former boss and that he was really happy with your work.

<u>Theory and practice</u>

The answers in the Question and Answer section are done in a relatively informal way. They have been crafted to include heavy PM theory, but the idea is to mix the PM theory or "textbook answer" with a real-life experience. If your answer is just a repeat of the textbook's answer, you may not sound real.

Body Language

Your body language can convey a stronger message than your words. Proper body language is critical in business situations. Your entrance, handshake and eye contact all make an impression.

A confident entrance is a good start to any business situation. When entering someone's office, check your posture, hold your head up, make eye contact and smile. Always initiate the handshake to make you appear more in control. Handshakes are often an indicator of a person's frame of mind, so practice your handshake and be conscious of the handshake you receive.

Maintain eye contact. It is important in our culture to look at the person to whom you are speaking approximately 80% of the time. Americans place a high value on eye contact and generally interpret it as a gesture of trust and confidence. During an interview, make eye contact when you are talking - particularly when making an important point - as well as when you are listening. Nodding is another gesture of support and agreement and is a good complement to eye contact.

If you are interviewed by a group, be especially careful to look at every person when answering a question. You should mostly be looking towards the person who asked the question but you should pan around the room to let people know that you are talking to them too.

Before your interview, practice your body language with someone you know and with whom you feel comfortable. Analyze your strengths and weaknesses to determine what you can do to improve. You may need to brush up on these points for your job search, but they will be tools you will need throughout your career.

Above all, remember that your positive attitude is critical and that positive nonverbal behavior naturally results from that kind of attitude. Your verbal and nonverbal communication will then be congruent, and your message received as you intend it.

Before the Interview

> Have directions to the interview, and allow plenty of time for travel and parking.
> Arrive 10 - 15 minutes early.
> Bring extra copies of your resume, your reference list, a good quality pen or pencil and a notepad.
> Consider bringing samples of your work that demonstrate your skills and abilities.
> Know the name and title of the person you are meeting.
> Research the company and the position. Know what qualities the employer requires.
> Practice answering questions and have a list of questions to ask the employer.
> Be prepared to answer tough questions.

During the Interview

> Greet the employer with a firm handshake and use his or her name.
> Maintain good eye contact and posture.
> Smile!
> Be alert and attentive. Show enthusiasm!
> Answer the questions asked. If you don't understand a question, ask for clarification.
> Emphasize your strong points by showing a match between what you offer and what they are looking for.

- Know your resume and be able to discuss every item listed.
- Never criticize a former employer, teacher, colleague or school.
- Follow the interviewer's lead. Allow periods of silence if the interviewer needs to think.
- Use proper grammar. Avoid nervous habit sounds such as like, um, uh, yeah, you know.
- Avoid discussing salary or benefits during the first interview unless a job offer is made (and even then, defer this).

Questions to Ask the Job Interviewer

Copy this list and take it with you to the interview.

- Can you describe a typical day for someone in this position?
- What is the top priority of the person who accepts this job?
- What are the day-to-day expectations and responsibilities of this job?
- How will my leadership responsibilities and performance be measured? By whom? How often?
- Can you describe the company's management style?
- Can you discuss your take on the company's corporate culture?
- What are the company's values?
- How would you characterize the management philosophy of this organization? Of your department?
- What is the organization's policy on transfers to other divisions or other offices?
- Are lateral or rotational job moves available?
- Does the organization support ongoing training and education for employees to stay current in their fields?
- What do you think is the greatest opportunity facing the organization in the near future? The biggest threat?
- Why did you come to work here? What keeps you here?
- How is this department perceived within the organization?
- Is there a formal process for advancement within the organization?
- What are the traits and skills of people who are the most successful within the organization?

Closing the Interview in a Great Way

When the interview is about to end, the interviewer will invite you to ask questions, and you must have questions prepared.

Preparation is critical. Make notes and write down questions you want to ask prior to the interview. Questions should be specific to the job and company. At the end of the interview, open your notebook to be sure that you have asked all your questions. You will be sending several positive messages about your work habits. It will show that you prepared for the interview, you take notes and follow through, and that you had an agenda you are following.

There is a list of general questions to ask later in this chapter. Copy the list and take it with you to the interview. But, there is one question you should always ask, and it can clinch the job for you. It is, "Have you found any area of my experience that you consider a weakness for this job? If you tell me what it is, I can try to address it." This is a great question because it forces the interviewer to name a weakness, and it gives you the chance to try to overcome any objection they might have.

Another way to ask the same question is to say something like "Do you have any question or concern about my ability to handle the work?"

Finally, Ask for the job!. You can say something like this:

"I want you to know that I am very interested in this position. I'm confident I can more than meet your expectations. How do you see me fitting into your team? "

Questions and Answers

I have seen firsthand candidates who had a good resume who got stumped by a question they could not answer. The result is an uncomfortable silence. The interviewee may say something to avoid the silence, but it is obvious that he/she is grasping to say anything that will make some sense. If a candidate gets stumped on just one question, the chances of moving to the next phase are reduced substantially.

When reading the following questions, practice formulating an answer or at least think about how you might answer it. Avoiding being blindsided by a question could mean the difference between being offered a job or not.

How to read the question and answer section

After a few years of work, resumes of people start to become very unique. It is not possible to give winning answers to interview questions that do not take into account the specifics of the job and the specifics of the candidate's experience and background. Nevertheless, we can offer you the next best thing.

Some of the answers below will have generic placeholders like *XYZ, x, y, z,* in italics. Put the particulars of your experience and background where you see those placeholders.

For instance, the job description might look like this:
"Project Manager needed to work on large Java projects."

If our answer is:
    "I have *x* years of experience programming with *XYZ.*"

So if you have five years of experience with Java, you would say:
    "I have five years of experience programming with Java."

In addition, sometimes when referring to the details of the job description, we will say something like (insert job description item here).

Preparation for the Job Interview – One More Time

There are several things that are going on in an interview. The more you prepare in advance, the less you will have to think on your feet during the interview and the better you will do. By preparing stories and answers ahead of time, you will have a much better chance to look professional, collected and ready to work.

Preparation is the key. Stories and answers must be memorized and their delivery should be practiced. You can then concentrate on the other elements of the interview, ask questions that tell you more about the job and relate relevant stories to what you are being told.

Section 2   Generic Interview Q & A

Most job interviews start with some icebreakers and some generic questions that may not relate specifically to project management. Some of those questions and answers are included here to give you a more complete perspective on the interview.

You must use the first and second questions to start selling yourself by including references to job skills, job descriptions, the industry or held positions that closely relate to the job at hand. Many hiring decisions are made on the first minutes of the interview. If you don't address what they want in the first few minutes, you may have broken the ice, but you lost the chance to make any points.

2.1   Tell Me About Yourself

Despite the deceptive phrasing, "Tell me about yourself," is not a request for your life story. The question you really need to answer is, "Why should I hire you?" Knowing this, your goal is to craft a convincing statement that will make the interviewer want to know more about you and what you can do for the company. You can count on having this question in your interview, so you must have a two-minute well-rehearsed answer.

This question can be answered in two parts. The first part is a 20-second summary that introduces you at a high level. If you have a summary at the top of your resume with your skills and experience, you can start with that. For example,

> "I am a project manager with x years of experience. I have been involved in *XYZ* projects for z years. My experience has been mostly around *xx* projects. I have a *XYZ* certification and my academic background is *xxx*." You can then add some statements about your personal qualifications. For instance, "I am a results-oriented person who interacts well with people. I like to set goals and keep them."

The second part will start with a mini-biography that should include your academic background, positions you have had, prior employers and projects you have worked on. Those elements are the framework to show that you have the skills and experience for this particular job.

As you describe your jobs and positions, you must highlight the work you did that is relevant to the job at hand. You should also highlight the use of certain skills that were mentioned in the job ad or job description and mention promotions and successful projects in which you participated. Don't get into much detail on a single job or project. Keep it at a high level.

To prepare, you must develop a response tailored to the specific employer and address its interests, goals and needs. You should revise, refine and rehearse your script until you can deliver it flawlessly – with energy, enthusiasm and confidence.

Your two-minute statement must show you to be a positive, contributing person, and it really depends on your own experience. Here is a simple model:

> "My academic background is in *business management,* and my first job was doing *xxx* for an *yyy* company. In that job, I learned to work in a team and was promoted to *zzz*. I went on to work for *XZY* where I was responsible for *xxx* and started using project management methodology. It was at that job where I learned (*insert job description item here*) and was very successful at it."

End with the question, "Is there anything I have mentioned that you would like me to go into in more detail?"

This is a great way to talk about what the other person would like to hear. If the interviewer asks you to just continue, take your history into the job that most closely relates to the job you are applying for. "OK, let me tell you what I did in the project *XYZ*."

2.2 Why did you leave XYZ Company?

State your reason for leaving honestly and succinctly and prepare responses for leaving other jobs you have had. If you were laid off, you can say something along this order:

> "The company had to adjust to market conditions and restructured. In the process, a good number of positions were eliminated, including mine. I am proud of the work I did there, and I will be able to use the experience I acquired there in this position. For example, I did a lot of *xxx* that I understand you use here."

2.3 Which of your jobs did you like best? Why?

Here is your chance to tell the interviewer about the specific areas in which you can be of most value in this organization. If you are noncommittal or vague in your response, it may suggest that you lack drive and the ability to analyze or plan for your own growth. It is normal to have preferences, but you must be careful. Everything you say can be used against you, so you should always be positive in your responses.

Some good answers:

- "I liked working at *XYZ Company* because I felt that I contributed and my bosses recognized it, too."

- "I liked *XYZ* because I learned a great deal about project management from the classes I was able to attend and also from my boss who had several years of experience. Another important element of that job was that I was in charge of (*insert job description item here*), which I really like because I think I am good at it."

- "I liked *XYZ* because I learned the power of teamwork."

Notice how you must pack your answer with useful information. For instance, you are saying that you learned from your boss, and this is a great trait to have. Hiring managers want the people who work for them to look at them as sources of knowledge. Another skill that is highly sought after is the ability to work on teams.

What <u>not</u> to say:

"I liked *XYZ* because the pay was good."

2.4   How did you get your past jobs?

Your reply will give an indication of your resourcefulness. If you can say that you found your job through networking, say so. Obtaining work through networking is proof that you have communication skills and can use a social network.

The not-so-great answer is, "I posted my resume on Monster/Dice/Yahoo/etc. and waited for recruiters to call me." This could be misinterpreted that you didn't take this most important matter into your own hands.

2.5   Why are you so interested in our company?

If "money" is your honest answer, you will probably be passed over. The question is an attitude indicator that may strongly influence the interviewer's image of you. Your answer also indicates how much you have researched the company.

This is one of those questions that require you to make connections to what you have done. You can use the company or the industry to show that you have already done the same kind of work, and that working for this company or industry would not be too different from what you have done before (at least in your eyes).

The best answer to this question involves talking about some specifics of the company, and you can only do that if you have done some research on it. A good source of information is recently published press releases. No matter how bad the prospects are for a company, their press releases will have a positive spin. That spin should be part of your response. A good answer is:

"In doing research for this position, I looked at the company information and it seems that things are looking good because (*insert press release spin here*). The industry itself is in line with the kind of position I would like."

It is much more difficult to gain insight and outlook for a private company. You might find some information, but nothing really insightful. You could say:

> "I am interested in working for a growing company like yours, because in a growing company my contributions will be easily recognized. Also, I can contribute in more than one area, and I think there would be opportunities to wear more than one hat."

Notice that you are not only answering the question but also sending strong messages about your willingness to contribute and your ability to be versatile. Both are sought-after traits by hiring managers.

This is a great opportunity to ask a good question:

> "What do you think attracts people to work and stay here?"

2.6   Why are you so interested in this particular job?

A good answer is:

> "I am pursuing this opportunity because my experience and interests very closely match the job description, requirements and the company. I would like to continue being successful in my career, and I am positive that I will be successful at this position because I have the skills you are looking for. I not only can do the job but will enjoy doing it."

You can ask:

> "Why would you think somebody would like to do this job?"

2.7   What are your long-range and short-range plans?

This has to be one of the most feared questions for most people. The interviewer wants to see if your plans mesh or conflict with the organization plans, and if your goals are realistic.

I gave the following answer in an interview over 15 years ago and was told that my answer to the question is what impressed them the most. My answer was, "I want to make $100,000 in five years." (It took me much longer than that to get to $100K.)

I would not advise you to give this answer without some qualifiers. A better answer is:

> "I would like to keep doing what I have been doing, which is to work on *xzy,* and keep increasing the responsibility of the jobs held in this line of work so that I will be making $*X* in five years."

The dollar amount that you mention should be between 50% and 75% more than the pay of the job you are applying for, and five is a good number of years. While you are talking about money, which is not always positive, you are also talking concrete figures, which is a very good thing.

The job or industry you mention (*xzy*) must be something that you have done before and also includes the job you are applying for. If you are changing lines of work, you have to have a very compelling history that would make sense. What you cannot say is some goal that is clearly incompatible with the job. A good question, at this point and one that can tell you a lot about the company would be:

> "I know you are hiring for (*insert job title here)* and I would be glad to do that job, but could you tell me if there would be opportunities for advancement?"

2.8   If you had complete freedom, what job would you choose?

Your answer is an indicator of your suitability for the organization. If you have arrived at the interview through a well thought-out zeroing in process, your ideal will most likely mesh with the real strengths you are presenting – and with what this company most likely needs. This is a tricky question. The best way to answer is:

> "I would like to work at a job where I can use my (*insert job description item here)* skills and keep learning more. I would like to be able to contribute and be appreciated for my contributions."

2.9   What are your top strengths?

The ability to talk knowledgeably about your strengths is an indication of healthy self-confidence. This is a good opportunity to verbalize your strengths backed by your accomplishments – strengths in action.

Remember that providing an example is important for these kinds of questions. You can say:

> "I work well with people, am a self-starter, and I find ways to get the job done. In my last project, I looked for opportunities to have some time outside regular work hours to learn more about the people in the office and at work. I teamed up with like-minded individuals I met in my initial training sessions and developed a network with them."

2.10 What are your weaknesses?

This is a "fishing" question. It tells the interviewer about your outlook and aptitudes. This question is your opportunity to briefly describe a less-than-favorable situation that you learned from or overcame. Turn it into a discussion of an accomplishment. Also, a weakness could be a knowledge deficiency that can easily be remedied by additional training, reading or experience, so relate your plan to address it. A good answer is:

> "It seems that *XYZ* technology is being used more and more and is here to stay. I have started reading the basics of it, and I would like to learn more about it."

You may find that some interviewers, especially human resources personnel, will not let go as easily and might insist on eliciting a real weakness with questions like, "Anything else? Any other weakness?" You may need to have another "weakness" ready to be "confessed" to satisfy their questioning.

If you have been working for a few years after college, you can say something that has worked for some people that were a few years into their careers.

> "I worked very hard in college, and I think I used my time wisely and learned a lot, as proven by the first job I had after school. But I did not go to an Ivy League school, and I think that could be seen as a weakness by some employers."

You must not show bitterness. On the contrary, you must show a good attitude about it and show that you have to work a little harder now. This answer can also be used if asked about the biggest mistake of your life.

Section 3   Project Management Interview Q & A

<u>How to use this section</u>

The purpose of this section is to give you the questions that you will be asked to prove that you have knowledge and experience in project management. Not all the questions will be asked of all people. If you are a beginner-level project manager, they may not ask you general management questions as much as questions about project management theory.

The answers given here are the basis for the response, and each is a bare bones answer over which you should add your own words. In some cases, you can take the answer and repeat it word for word, and it would be a good answer. In most cases, you should add your own experience as well as specific project names, specific situations, etc.

You should go through the questions and answers and dress them with your own experience. Doing this is critical to the job interview preparation so that you will be ready and rehearsed to answer the questions in the interview.

3.1   Can you tell me about a problem you encountered while managing a project and how you dealt with it?

The purpose for the question is to assess your problem-solving skills and ability to get the job done even if there are problems. These are the characteristics of a good project manager. After all, anybody can "manage" if there are no problems.

Your answer must include creativity and show that you are a problem solver. It is better if the problem and the solution do not include personal conflicts but problems related to technical difficulties or time and cost constraints. It is much better if you did not create the problem in the first place! A sample answer:

> "I was put in charge of an already-in-progress project because it was in danger of failing to meet the deadline. I talked with members of the team and determined that the critical path was passing by the design and development of some enhancements that needed to be done, but were far from being completed. I created a project schedule with MS Project, identified the enhancements that could be done with the resources available and delivered on the promised date. I presented the plan to the users. They accepted it, and we executed it. We delivered on time. The user was happy, and I was commended for my work."

To answer a question like this you should know the basic steps for problem resolution:

1. Define the problem
2. Gather information until enough data has been gathered or it is not practical to find out more
3. Identify a solution and alternatives
4. Evaluate each alternative
5. Choose a solution
6. Implement the solution

Potential follow-up questions:

"In this company, are deadlines set in stone for most projects?"

"How does this company go about setting deadlines for projects?"

3.2   How do you handle disruptive team members?

This question provides proof for your handling of real-life situations. A good way to establish that you have experience handling disruptive team members is by starting with something like this:

"Throughout my career, I have had to deal with disruptive team members and have come to the belief that 'if there were no problem people, there would be no need for people who solve problems'."

Then you can go with one of the following sample answers.

"If the team member is not behaving up to standards, I look to make a corrective action as soon as practically possible. The sooner it's done the better, because the earlier the intervention, the easier the solution. For instance, in the project XYZ, one of the team members became a persistent complainer. He would criticize the users, and would tell everybody the users were wrong or that the analysts were wrong. He was impacting the morale of the project.

I told my boss what was happening and how I planned on handling it. Then I set up a meeting with the team member and explained to him that the comments he made might be justified or not, but the way the comments were expressed was impacting the morale of the team and my ability to get the job done as requested by the client.

I asked him to talk to me in private about his concerns. I was clear in telling him that the users could be given feedback through the analysts, but he must let the users and the business analysts determine what needed to be done, and let them learn from their mistakes, if needed. He could alert them of issues, but if not heard, there was no need to keep raising the same issues again and again.

I explained this in detail to him and made sure he understood the problem and what I wanted him to do from then on. I also made sure he recognized that what I was asking was reasonable."

A second sample answer:

"I meet one-on-one with the team member and discuss the disruptive behavior in no personal terms. I go to lengths to discuss the behavior, not the person. I start by stating the behavior, and I describe the impact of the behavior on the project and request specific changes. I outline the consequences of not changing and obtain a commitment to reduce or eliminate the behavior."

A third sample answer:

"As a project manager, I look to identify the source for the disruptive behavior. In my experience, the reason is usually one of the following:

- Lack of skill in the job
- Personal problems outside of work
- Low motivation
- Lack of job structure
- Incompatibility between employee and employer
- Inadequate supervision
- Emotional immaturity
- Physiological deterioration or poor health

I describe the behavior and how it affects the work of the person and other team members. I listen for any clear indication of where the problem might lie. I might try to help within my area of influence, but I mostly look for a commitment to change. If a commitment is not obtained, I evaluate the need to escalate the issue. I may recommend a course of action, including the removal of the team member from the project."

Project Management Theory around Disruptive Behavior:

> The PM's job responsibility is to get the job done, and while support and understanding can be given, the nonproductive behavior must be compared against expectations.
> The PM must know the human resource policies.
> The PM must practice active listening.
> The PM must take notes to document disruptive behavior and support disciplinary action.
> The PM must be prepared to handle disruptive team members. This is a key element of their work. They cannot start a project wishing that everybody would just do their job.
> The PM is not a psychologist.

3.3   How do you handle nonproductive team members?

"When I give assignments to team members, I make sure it is clear what the work product standards will be and what the timeline will be. I also establish weekly touch-base sessions.

If the team member is not performing up to standards, I look to make a corrective action as soon as practically possible. The sooner it's done the better, because the earlier the intervention, the easier the solution.

My weekly touch-base meetings will help me uncover early issues around nonperformance. If I see that the team member is not performing, I will talk about the work products and not about the person.

When I discuss nonperformance or lack of productiveness, I use the techniques of the *One-minute Manager* where the behavior or action is discussed, not the person.

1. Define the nonperformance in objective and specific terms (e.g., the functional description is supposed to have use cases, and there is none).
2. Describe the impact of the nonperformance on the project.
3. Specify the required changes.

4. Outline the consequences.
5. Agree on a plan and time to get back to expected performance standards.

As a project manager, I look to identify the source of the nonperformance. The plan to get back on track would be based on the identified source of the lack of performance.

Most of the reasons behind lack of performance are:

- Lack of knowledge of the standards expected
- Lack of skill in the job
- Morale, motivation and personal issues

If I don't see that the team member will get up to speed in a reasonable amount of time, I will escalate the issue."

3.4 How do you motivate team members who are burned out or bored?

This is a question that cannot be answered quickly as motivation is a big discipline unto itself. Nevertheless, the question comes up often in job interviews because most people need to be motivated on a continuous basis. Below are some suggested answers for each situation.

Burned out team members

"As a project manager, I may not have direct influence on people's salaries, but I can provide other non-monetary rewards that team members appreciate."

"The best way to handle burn-out is to prevent it, but once it happens or if I come into a project where I see burn-out symptoms, my first step is to identify the reasons."

"Burn-out usually comes from job ambiguity, low job ability or dissatisfaction with the work environment."

"To assess the situation, it is best to check that the team member understands the job description. If it is understood, perhaps the skills to handle the job are lacking. If the skills exist, perhaps there is very low motivation to do the job."

Job ambiguity

"If the job is not clearly defined to the team member, it might be a good idea to go over the responsibilities and discuss tactic approaches to do the job. This should give the team member a head start."

Low job ability

"If the team member does not have the skills, he might be overworking himself/herself and not producing the right results. Training or close guidance should be the solution here."

Dissatisfaction with the work environment

"This could be internal or external to the project. The team member might be dissatisfied with his work environment and his perspectives with the firm even if the project succeeds. The traditional motivation techniques should be used here. "

Boredom

"Boredom is easier to handle as there is always more work to do. But before handing additional work, I discuss the situation with the team member and discuss the need to do topnotch work in his/her current assignment. I then give them other work that might be more interesting."

3.5   How do you motivate people?

"Different people have different motivations. It is important to know what motivates each of the team members and select assignments and motivation techniques based on each individual.

There are several things that I do as a project manager to motivate team members. I start by creating a positive team environment by using several techniques.   I promote enthusiasm and optimism by sharing my own enthusiasm and optimism and highlight the job's importance.   There is always an aspect of the project that makes it unique and desirable. I highlight the uniqueness of the project and the experience that the team members are gaining.

I believe that challenges are good motivators.   I pick an achievable challenge and make sure it's overcome. I give clear job descriptions and clear standards to go by. In my experience, people work better if they know what they are supposed to do and how they fit into the overall picture. I also expend some time in team-building exercises and do one-on-one meetings with team members to check on progress. Most importantly, I look for early signs of trouble or lack of motivation.

I reward team members with:

Praise
I thank and recognize the team members when they do good work, which is most of the time.

Involvement
I motivate team members by involving them in decision-making when their input is requested.

Autonomy and authority
Most employees value being given the freedom to do their work as they best see fit. The ultimate form of recognition for many employees is to have increased autonomy and authority. I give autonomy and authority to team members as incentive to do their best. I am also aware that I must be tolerant when somebody is given a new assignment and does not do it as well as I would have done it.

Learning and development
Employees highly value learning opportunities. The opportunity to learn and practice new skills is a good motivator. As a PM, I discuss with the team members what their learning interests might be and give assignments based on that input."

3.6 How do you handle team members who come to you with their personal problems?

"I listen attentively and with empathy, understanding that I am not a counselor. I ask questions and let the person develop the solution him/herself. I will also ask if I can be of help or if the person needs time to deal with those issues.

If the employee asks for a break in his/her workload because of the personal problems, if it within my authority, I would consider giving him/her time to work through those personal issues, but he/she must understand that performance must go back to normal at some point in time.

I would leave serious problems to professional counselors or even social services as needed."

3.7 Explain how you operate interdepartmentally.

"When working with other departments, I am careful to communicate at the right level. Normally, a project manager does not have the authority to request work or collaboration from other departments, and it must be done through careful coordination. Most likely, I will request that the project sponsor request the help of the other department. Once the contact has been established, any work assignment has to be cleared with the individual's supervisor. If I obtain a commitment of work to be done, then I involve the supervisor in critical communications."

3.8 Tell me how you would react to a situation where there was more than one way to accomplish the same task, and there were very strong feelings by others on each position.

"If possible, compromise on a solution that uses both positions. I would have the team agree on a method to evaluate the benefits of each solution. I would then compare those alternatives against the agreed upon evaluation method. This way the issue becomes less personal and egos are not bruised.

For instance, in a project at *XYZ*, I was the project manager and we had to select a software package. The packages were really very similar, but the team members had very strong opinions about which to choose. I used a matrix of factors where every consideration discussed was included. We then proceeded to give different weights to the factors without thinking of the specific solution. Once the factors and the weights were identified, we analyzed each software product in light of each factor and gave it a score. The group agreed that the highest score reflected the best option and no egos were bruised."

3.9 What is your management style?

You must show that you recognize that there are different management styles and that you have one. The three management styles are: autocratic (directive), hands-off (paternalistic) and democratic (participative). The paternalistic and participative models are considered good models for most situations involving teams of highly skilled members. There is also the situational leadership theory that has definitive benefits, and this theory says that different leadership styles are better in different situations and that leaders must be flexible enough to adapt their style to the situation they are in.

It would be interesting to have an idea of the management style of the company or person that is interviewing you and if you can adapt, make sure to mention that style. A suggested answer:

> "I believe that the management style must meet the project and the situation. In general, I favor a participatory style, but if the project has a deadline rapidly approaching, I will move to a more directive role.
>
> I think that most people respond better to a participative style, where they have a chance to be heard. This improves the output and motivation of the team. I believe that most people meet high performance expectations if appropriately motivated and have a supportive environment.
>
> I think that most people are creative, imaginative, ambitious and committed to meeting the organization's goals. As a PM, my role is to direct that energy towards the project goals. I also believe that most people are self-disciplined, can direct and control themselves, desire responsibilities, and accept them willingly."

Follow-up question:

> "Could you tell me, what is the favored management style in this company?"

3.10 What do you look for when you hire people?

Most employers seem to agree that good employees display qualities such as dependability, punctuality, initiative, a positive attitude toward the job, ability to get along well with others, flexibility, motivation, organization and the ability to perform assigned duties. Keeping this in mind, a good answer is:

> "Besides the skills specific for the job, I look to hire a person who would fit in with the organization's culture. I look for flexibility, initiative, energy and a desire to move up in the organization."

3.11 Give me an example of your leadership involvement where teamwork played an important role.

Teamwork is critical to project execution. You will want to show your ability to solicit ideas from others, listen carefully and persuade people to your point of view. One of the benefits of teamwork is that a team can conceive of ideas that a single person would not. Teamwork does foster creativity. Your answer, reflecting these ideals, could be:

> "In the project *XYZ*, we were charged with creating business processes for a brand new company. I was the project manager and no one on the team had done that kind of work before. By using our diverse backgrounds and working together, we came up with all the processes and procedures that were needed. For instance, I knew the processes needed at a high level, but I have never detailed a process flow. Some of the team members had experience with doing detail process flows but did not know about the industry. Other team members knew about the software we were going to use but did not know how to write rules and procedures."

Follow-up question: "How are teams created here?"

3.12 How do you start a project?

The ability to start a project is critical, and it is more difficult to start one than to take over an existing project. The absolute keyword in your answer here must be *planning*.

> "Specific methodologies may change, but the first steps I take in starting a project are:
>
> 1. Identify the business sponsors
> 2. Identify the resources initially assigned to the project
> 3. Create the initial project charter and an initial timeline
> 4. Create a short-term plan to get initial activities scheduled
> 5. Proceed to complete the first version of the project plan
>
> The challenge that every project initially faces is that all people involved are ready to jump into action, but in order to be effective, not have false starts or get going on the wrong path, one must do some planning before people get in motion. I try to do at least a two-week plan to make sure participants are doing work that is conducive to the

final product. Then I take those two weeks to do a long-term plan and a detailed plan for the next few weeks."

You can ask: "How a project is officially started here?"

3.13　What are the basic components of a project plan?

"The components of a project plan must match the magnitude of the project, and it should include the following, either as individual documents or as part of an integrated project plan document:

- Project charter
- Project management approach
- Scope statement
- Work Breakdown Structure (WBS)
- Responsibility chart/assignments
- Network diagram
- Major milestones
- Budget
- Schedule
- Resources
- Change control system/plan
- Performance measurement baselines
- Management plans (scope, schedule, cost, quality, staffing, communications, risk response, procurement)"

If the company has a written methodology, then the management plans are in the methodology so they don't have to be repeated here.
You can also ask: "Could you tell me if you have project plans and if so, what do they cover?"

Another good question is: "Do you have a written methodology that talks about management plans?"

3.14　If you are teaching the ropes to a new Project Manager, what would you say are the most important things he needs to look for?

This question measures your experience and the ability to synthesize your knowledge. This is a good answer:

"I would say, 'Have a project charter and commitment from the project sponsor, then plan the work and work the plan. Keep a close eye on communications, issue management, risk management and scope.' I would also advise him/her on key documents to keep: Project Charter, Project Plan and Project Schedule, Activity-responsibility matrix, RTVM (Requirements Traceability Verification Matrix), and Final Sign-off."

3.15 What would be the key artifacts needed in a project?

"In my opinion, the key artifacts of a project are:

- Project Charter
- Project Plan
- Work Breakdown Structure
- Activity-responsibility matrix
- Status report
- Issue list
- Risk tracking
- RTVM (Requirements Traceability Verification Matrix)
- Final Sign-off"

3.16 How do you manage change?

Change control is the management process for requesting, reviewing, approving, carrying out and controlling changes to the project's deliverables. Change control is usually applied once a document or phase has been completed and signed off by the appropriate stakeholders. Change will happen in a project and must be managed.

Not long ago, and in two different interviews, I heard an answer to this question that I think was wrong because it left out the most important things. One of the candidates had several years of experience and a PMP certification, and the other had only some project management experience, but it was interesting to see that both had the same answer. The answer is wrong because it addresses only a small part of the overall change control.

The wrong answer was: "I manage change by keeping an updated project plan. This way, when changes are discussed, I can quickly assess the impact on the overall project timeline."

A much better answer is:

"Change is an important component of the lifetime of a project, and I dedicate time to manage it. I start change control at the beginning of the project by having a change control plan. This plan is a formal process to ensure that only authorized changes are made to the final work product. Team members must know what it will take to make a change.

The change plan I like to work with says that a pre-defined group of people will be empowered to authorize change. In small projects, it includes the change approvers in the activity-responsibility matrix. I have worked in projects where there was a group of people from the team that was the only group authorized to make certain changes. As the project moves along, each work product is base-lined when it is approved. If any stakeholder suggests a change to a base-lined document, the change is documented and given to the change control committee or to the group authorized to make a change in it. The change is adopted or rejected and documented, and the results communicated to the team.

What this means is that change control not only refers to changes made to the software, but change control includes changes done to all project artifacts created. For instance, if the project charter is approved and a change to the charter is proposed, it must go through the change control process. By planning and setting up a process for change control, changes do not derail the project."

3.17 How do you manage conflict in the project team?

This is a frequently asked question in a job interview, but it really does not have a simple answer. Being a project manager in a well-motivated, capable and conflict-free team is not a challenge, but real-life projects are rarely like that. Conflict management is a science in itself, and the question is just too broad.

The main reason to ask such a broad question is to see if the interviewee knows that conflict does occur and to see how the interviewee has confronted conflict successfully. Nevertheless, while you can start by saying that the best course of action depends on several circumstances, you are still expected to give some sort of answer. Since there are many kinds of conflict, you could ask:

"There are several kinds of conflict that can happen in a project. Do you have any specific type of conflict in mind?"

Like many other questions, the best way to answer this is by telling a specific example of how conflict was resolved and not try to do a lecture on how to address conflict.

One answer could be:

> "Conflict will happen in a project and I know that my role as a project manager is to eliminate the conflicts that will appear. If there is conflict between two team members, my first step is to isolate the conflict from the rest of the team. I meet with each party to the conflict individually and listen with an open mind.
>
> I think that the key to solving conflicts is to define issues without involving personalities. The idea here is that the focus should be on the needs of each team member as they pertain to the project.
>
> Most of the time, I will look for a win-win solution that would be accepted by both sides. In other cases, given time constraints or the importance of the issue, I may go ahead and be directive in the course of action, but this tends to be a win–lose situation, and I'd rather not go that way.
>
> I pay attention to early signs of conflict because I am aware that what I or other team members see as a minor issue could be seen as a big one by another member of the team.
>
> If I get involved in a conflict, I try to put my ego aside and work on finding positive solutions. I concentrate on outcomes, not personalities. That is exactly what I did in project *XYZ* where a team leader wanted to have one of the analysts removed in order to bring in another person. I heard what she had to say, and I involved a manager to supervise the work of the analyst in question. After a couple of weeks I talked with the manager and I saw no reason to make changes in the team but addressed the issues of perceived lack of capacity."

3.18   How do you deal with a difficult team member?

A project manager must be able to work with all the people in the organization. Each organization has its own set of difficult people who are still working there because they have some sought-after talent.

Before talking about a particular case, you could ask what kind of difficult people they would like for you to address. The answer will give you a good glimpse of the kind of work that you may encounter in this position. But if you do ask the question, you might be expected to describe how you would handle the situation. If you attempt to outline a response to the specific bad behavior, it is possible that your answer will appear wrong to the interviewer. Therefore, it is probably better to go with a rehearsed answer rather than trying to improvise on the spot. A good answer is:

> "Difficult people come in different forms, and each of them has to be treated in a different way. In general, I maintain professionalism and do not take the issue personally, even when the difficult person is attacking my work or my decisions. Above all, I still give the difficult person respect. Sometimes, that's all they are looking for. I don't try to push back using their own games as it is likely that I cannot be as good at it as they are.
>
> Dealing with difficult people is part of the job description and must be dealt with. Difficult behavior will not go away by itself. I don't like the fact that I, as project manager, have to divert my efforts to deal with the issue, but it must be done.
>
> I have had to deal with difficult people who were un-collaborative. One particular person would not share information with other team members. He would not even share books that were company property. It was a typical case of emotional immaturity. I resolved this conflict by recognizing and praising the work of this person in public while making sure everybody knew he had the source of the information.
>
> I had to document difficult behavior, and I did so in very specific and non-personal terms. I try to deal with behavior, not with persons. It makes for an easier resolution."

3.19   What qualifications are required to be an effective project manager?

This question is used to measure how comfortable you are with the qualities needed for a good project manager. The key to answering this question is not just to list some qualities, but also to show with an example that you possess those qualities. Remember that you have to sell yourself all the time and that you have to take advantage of the open nature of the questions to tout yourself. You can keep talking until you sense that the interviewer thinks it's enough.

Your answer could be:

"A good project manager must:
- Be organized
- Have good communication skills
- Pay attention to detail
- Be a self-starter and self-motivated
- Be a team player

I think I possess these qualities. I am organized; I have a place for everything and everything is in its place. I plan activities and coordinate events well. I have good communication skills and find ways to talk to people and maintain a conversation. I make friends and communicate ideas to superiors as well as to people working for me.

I pay attention to detail. For instance, I am good at proofreading documents. In my last job, I was usually the first one to find errors in training materials and software documentation.

My former employers would say that I am a self-starter and that I have initiative."

3.20 Your three-month project is about to exceed the projected budget after the first month. What steps will you take to address the potential cost overrun?

The question is exploring whether you know when to ask questions. The best answer is:

"The first step is to make sure the stakeholders are aware of the situation. The sooner they are informed, the better. The second step is to examine the reason for the cost overrun, evaluate alternatives and present them to management."

3.21 You are given the assignment of project manager and the team members have already been identified. To increase the effectiveness of your project team, what steps will you take?

Knowing team dynamics would help in answering this question and a good answer would be:

"I'll find the strengths and weaknesses of the team members before I confirm assignments and estimate durations. I will have one-on-one conversations with each team member to find their personal interests. I will then look to align the project goals with the goals of each team member."

3.22 You have been assigned as the project manager for a team comprised of new employees just out of college and "entry-level" consulting staff. What steps can you take to insure that the project is completed against a very tight time deadline?

Remember that when answering hypothetical questions of "what if" scenarios, it is much better to say, "What I did was…" versus "What I'd do…."

"I have been in this particular situation in project *XYZ*. What I did was to find the strengths and weaknesses of the team members from their supervisors. I then talked with them one-on-one to get their input about their experience or academic skills. I then identified training needs and allocated time for training. Training, in the context of this project, was just a day or two. I also paired team members to complement strengths and to have one learn from the other."

3.23 What is the difference between a project plan and a project schedule? What do you include in a project schedule?

"The project plan is the collection of the plans of the project, and it includes other documents like the project charter. It is actually a living document that will keep growing as the project gets executed.

The project schedule lists the tasks, the timing in which those tasks are going to occur, when each task will be executed and sometimes the people executing the tasks. The project schedule is usually done with a tool like Microsoft Project."

Project schedules vary from company to company. So a good question at this time is: "How do you set up project schedules here?"

3.24 How do you track a project?

If you answer "earned value," you would not say what most hiring managers want to hear. This is a better answer:

> "I track three main aspects of a project: the planned activities, the open issues, and the open risks. I track planned activities by discussing the progress with each team member. I usually track advancement by indicating 25, 50, 75 and 100% completion.

> I also track open issues. Open issues must have an owner and a reporting date. I discuss the open issue progress with the issue owner.

> I also track and monitor risks. I ask the team for risk awareness and reporting. I discuss risk status with the assigned risk owner. I keep track of risk probability and risk impact as they can change over time.

> I put the tracking status in a status report and then confirm this in a status meeting. I also like to have an overall status indicator for the project, something like green, yellow, red. Green means we are on target, yellow means something is putting the timing of the project at risk, and red means that the target date will be missed."

Some companies still don't make a distinction between risks and issues. You could ask a question like this: "Do you track risks and issues in different artifacts?" Or you could ask, "Could you tell me how you track risks?" Another question could be, "Are project statuses consolidated somewhere on an executive dashboard?"

By asking these questions, you are elevating the discussion from project tracking to a more advanced stage.

3.25 How do you track risks? Tell me about the risks your last project had.

The specific risks that you identified in your last project will tell a lot about the project and your project involvement. You should answer:

> "I use an Excel spreadsheet where I list the risk, the date it was created, the probability that it will occur, the impact on the project, the response to it and the owner of the risk. I review open risks during the status meeting and track changes, like actions or responses, changes in probability of occurrence or changes on impact, and during my status meeting, I encourage team members to discuss potential risks.

In my last project, the biggest risk was that we could not find enough *Java* developers with enough time to code the applications. Another risk was that another department, whose data we needed to receive, might not have been able to provide the data ahead of a major hardware upgrade they were going to do.

Yet another risk was that we might not have been able to hire the head of a department in time so that the project would not be delayed."

Some questions that will tell you where the company is regarding risk management: "Are project managers here asked to track risks on a weekly basis?" "Are risks part of the status report?"

3.26   What is the difference between a risk and an issue?

People who are new to project management confuse the terms and some can even have strong opinions about them. Here is the best answer:

"I have noticed in talking with people in different organizations that there are different opinions about these topics. The textbook answer is that "risk" is a potential problem that may impact the project in terms of cost, time or quality. Project Management Theory even says that a risk could have a positive or negative impact. The response to risk can be mitigation, avoidance, acceptance and guidance for response control.

The textbook definition of "issue" is a problem that has actually occurred in the project and must be addressed.   Risks can become issues."

Once you state your answer, the interviewer may want to argue with you about the response. Don't argue. If you feel that you need to respond to the argument, you could say: "Yes, this area was discussed in my prior job as well. We agreed that the important point was that everybody used the same definition."

You could ask if your definition matches the company's definition.

3.27   How do you define quality in project management?

"Quality is a word used in everyday speech that has one clear definition in the project management context. Quality is the degree to which a system or work product meets standards and/or requirements."

As with other questions, the interviewer may object to your definition and may try to argue with you. Do not fall for it. If you argue with the interviewer, your chances of getting the job reduce to near zero. If the interviewer comes back with a different answer you could reply:

> "Yes, I think that is a good definition. This has been a point of discussion in training classes and at work. I believe that it is important that everybody shares the same definition.
>
> I think the reason we have so many definitions of quality is that quality is a relatively new concept in project management. The concepts of quality that we are using come from manufacturing, with Six Sigma being a good example. Also, another issue that clouds the discussion about quality is that sometimes it refers to the quality of the process, i.e.: How good is the project management? Is it up to standards? And sometimes it refers to the quality of the final product, i.e.: How good are the artifacts produced by the process?"

Follow-up questions:

> "Do you follow Six Sigma principles?"

> "Do you encourage employees to pursue Six Sigma certifications?"

Six Sigma is a discipline based on quality, and it is a good thing to mention when quality is mentioned. There is a good definition of Six Sigma in Part 2, Section 8.3.

3.28 What is the difference between quality management and quality control?

Quality management is done throughout the project's life cycle. Quality control is done at sporadic times to make sure the product and the process are meeting standards.

3.29 At what time in the project do you start quality control?

The concepts of quality control and quality management, and even quality planning, are not uniform in the corporate world. The best way to answer this question is by recognizing that some definitions must be done first, and making clear that quality control starts at the beginning of the project.

"I have noticed that in some places the definitions of quality management and quality control need to be clarified. In general, quality management is done throughout the project life cycle. Quality control is done at sporadic times to make sure the product and the process are meeting standards.

I start quality control early in the project. I believe in building quality into the product, not inspecting for quality at the end of the process. Quality must be verified for every single document created by the project, starting with the project charter."

Follow-up question:

"How do you define quality control?"

3.30 What would you say if a team member asks why project management is needed? Why do we have to do all this documentation ahead of the real work?

This is a very telling question. It is intended to measure several things. Do you actually believe in the project management process? Can you sell it to the team members? Would you follow direction from upper management that says that a process must be followed when the team members are not used to it or don't see value in it? A good answer to why project management in a given company is needed:

"It has been proven again and again that following a process improves the quality and reduces the cost and time that it takes to do a project. There are several studies that say that a great majority of projects actually fail and are not completed. A good project management process helps achieve a higher rate of success.

I would think most people agree that following a process and documenting the project are critical to a successful project. What might be up for discussion is how much process we apply to a particular project.

The process and documentation needed for that process have been defined by upper management and are based on company needs and best practices after seeing other projects fail. We follow this process because it is believed that it will help build quality products."

As to: "Why do we have to do all these documents ahead of the real work?" If somebody asks a question like this, I would suggest providing basic education on software development methodologies and project management.

> "The 'real work' *is* the documents that we are doing now. The project documents like the charter, requirements document and the rest are the real work since they actually define what the system is going to do. The code is one more document in the progression of building the system."

Follow-up question:

"How much software development methodology training or project management training do programmers receive in this company?"

3.31 What have you learned in obtaining your PMP that you are using in real-life projects?

The interviewer can learn a lot from the answer to this question, and it can be a difficult one to answer if you have not prepared for it. The emphasis in your answer has to be on anything new you learned that you have actually used afterwards.

> "When I prepared to obtain the PMP certification and saw all the different areas of knowledge, I recognized a good deal of them. There were also new concepts and tools. A lot of what I found were concepts that I had heard of, but it was nice to see them formalized, and it also validated that what I was doing before was not that different from project management as seen by PMI.

> While I knew about project scheduling, critical paths and project control, the areas that were new to me were Earned Value and Risk Management.

> I have not used Earned Value much, but I have used Risk Management since learning about it."

3.32 How do you make sure that outside companies meet their deadlines?

"Several steps must be taken to make sure contractors meet their deadlines, and many of them have to be done at the time of sourcing, negotiation and awarding contracts.

A contractor's progress must be followed even more closely than that of internal team members. A contractor's work is a project unto itself and must be documented as such. It must have an absolutely clear product description and must have contractually agreed upon responsibilities about reporting status.

I would make sure that the contract with the vendor makes the following elements clear:

- Vendor will provide a written status report on a weekly basis
- Status should include activities worked on, issues, and risks
- Vendor should follow proper project management principles
- Vendor can be asked to provide project plans, project schedules and resource assignments
- Vendor should attend a status meeting and provide answers to status questions

As happens with tasks assigned to internal team members, project delays and problems will be uncovered earlier if there are regularly established status reports and meetings. The key to preventing delays with contactors is through weekly (and sometimes daily) project tracking meetings to look for early signs of slips and other problems."

3.33 What do you do if a team member presents a work product that you know is flawed or incomplete, but the team member insists it is complete and sound?

This is a very political question. The "right" answer depends on the organization and the actual power that the project manager has. In a matrixed environment, you as a project manager have little power, and the team will question your knowledge of the subject matter.

Do not offer to fix it yourself – this might be the worst possible answer. But then again, it depends on the organization. Sometimes the PM is expected to cover for the team members.

A key part of the answer is sticking to procedures and emphasizing that you have acted in different ways in that regard following company policy or customs.

"I have run into this situation and have responded to it in different ways, depending on company policy.

If I am on the reviewer's group for the work product, I would write down my notes and back my observations with examples of other work products created in the firm or with quotes from the methodology or textbooks. I would try to make it as impersonal as possible and just refer to existing documentation or literature without trying to show off.

If the problem still persists and the team members that will use the artifact in the next phases don't see the problem, I would inform the team member's supervisor of the situation and arrange for training or support to be given so that the assignment can be completed.

If am not a reviewer, I would make sure that whoever is the reviewer actually reviews the work."

Follow-up question:

"As I said, I have run into this situation and responded in different ways. How would I handle it here?"

3.34 What would you do if a manager whose resources you are using keeps saying that all the documentation required by the project is getting in the way of actual progress?

"The methodology should provide for exceptions. I would let the manager request an exception to the methodology. After all, the PM is only enforcing the methodology he/she has been handed down.

It has been proven time and again that a good project management methodology reduces cost and time and improves quality. Still, it is often that some people will disagree with the level of process that the company has decided to exercise.

I believe that a good process actually helps the project and that the levels of process required vary by company. The challenge is to find the right level of process and to make sure that management agrees with the directives of upper management."

Follow-up question:

"Could you tell me how much process you have? Is the level of process supported by everybody?"

3.35 What was the CMM level at your current/last job?

You need to know the CMM levels to answer this question.

> "As a whole the company was probably at a level 2, but my projects were run at a higher level because of my personal commitment to improve processes. We have a defined process, but I was improving it over time."

A good follow-up: "What level do you think you are?"

3.36 Describe what you did in a difficult project environment to get the job done on time and on budget

Here we have another perfect example of a STAR response. There are broadly two kinds of issues in projects. One is the issues the project must resolve as part of the overall work breakdown structure. For instance, if the project is building a road, an issue inherent to the nature of the project would be to design a bridge that meets the requirements of weight and traffic and that is done at minimum cost. In other words, it should not be over-engineered.

In a computer project, an inherent issue is to write applications that meet online requirements such as having a response time less than a second or two.

The other set of problems that a project has comes not from the activities that were initially in the project plan, but problems arising from the human resources involved, the work environment, the external challenges, the unexpected occurrences, acts of God, etc.

While it could be argued that sometimes the distinction might be difficult to make, the bottom line is that the project manager must be able to manage the project through the second class of issues while the team members work on the first.

When answering questions about external challenges to the project, the project manager must show that he/she understands that those problems will always happen and that resolving them is everyday work.

"I have never been in a project where everything went according to plan. There are always challenges that come from different areas, and the project environment is one of them. I had a challenge when I was a team lead and my company was providing services to *xyz company it* turned out that the internal IT personnel appeared to have been sabotaging our work. They were not happy that an external consulting firm was doing the work they thought they were qualified to do. There were several things we had to do to address the situation, like making our own backups, helping the client assign unique passwords to all personnel and changing passwords used by the applications. I instructed my team to turn up the charm and go out of their way to make friends with the employees, and I think that getting closer to them on a personal basis helped as much or more than anything else to avoid more problems."

3.37 What was the biggest problem you faced on your last project? And how did you address it?

You have the opportunity to shine here if you tackle not task-related problems, but actual project management problems.

"I was the project manager for the project *XYZ,* and we were making good progress during the development phase. Then my boss announced a company-wide personnel reduction and said I would have to give up some of the people in my project to other projects. I had to do the best I could to meet the commitments to the users. I told my boss I would see that it was done and went to my project plan and reassigned resources. I gave more responsibility to two programmers and asked a senior analyst to supervise their analysis work. I also made other changes to the timeline. I did have to negotiate the postponing of the creation of two reports with the users, but they understood since they also had phased cuts."

3.38 What was your role in your last project?

This seemingly innocent question is to determine how much project management experience you actually have. If you are considered a project manager in your present job, your role would be that of a project manager. If your current role is not as a project manager, you should quickly mention what your current role is, and immediately mention the last project where you were a project manager, or at least a project lead.

"Before becoming a project manager, I did a lot of work doing programming in *XYZ*, and I am still considered an expert. When a need appeared about coding in *XYZ*, they asked me to help out with programming, and that's what I am doing now. Prior to that, my role has been that of a project manager."

3.39 What was the most interesting role you played in a project?

If the most interesting role you played in a project was not that of a project manager, perhaps you are not fit for the role.

3.40 What is the most common reason why projects fail?

The most frequent reason is poorly formulated requirements.

3.41 What do you do when a team member does not complete his/her assignment and has gone to another project?

The question is measuring your ability to deal with resource issues that will present themselves in projects. The important thing is to show that it will happen, and you will deal with it. Problems do happen and the project must continue.

> "As an experienced manager I might be able to complete some of the work, but most likely a specialist will be required. So I evaluate if the missing parts can be done on extra time or if a new resource can be brought up. This has actually happened to me at project *XYZ*, and I did exactly that."

3.42 Have you used Microsoft Project? How do you like it?

Watch out! This is a loaded question. Do not speak badly of Microsoft Project (MSP). MSP has had a set of problems in the past, but it works for a great variety of situations.

> "Yes, I have experience using Microsoft Project and have used it for the last five years. It is a great tool, and it has helped me manage and control projects."

3.43 How do you verify that the requirements identified for a project are actually included in the final delivery to the users?

Another format of this question is:

How do you verify that the requirements are correct and that they reflect what the users want?

"I have used an artifact called a requirements traceability matrix that lists the original requirements and tracks them through the diverse phases of analysis, technical design, programming, testing and acceptance by the user."

3.44 Are you detail-oriented or big-picture-oriented?

"While working on a project, I am detail-oriented, but I also make myself look at the big picture to see how my project fits in the big scale of things in the department and in the company."

3.45 Would you call yourself tough-minded and thick-skinned?

"I would not go as far as calling myself tough-minded and thick-skinned, but I think I have some of that in me, and that has helped me to be a good project manager. I have learned to be thick-skinned since I must be able to not take things personally and concentrate on getting the job done. I would call myself persistent and easy to work with."

3.46 What are your greatest strengths and weaknesses in the Project Management areas of knowledge?

You must know the Project Management areas of knowledge. (You can find them in Part 2 of this book)

You must assess your skills and be able to answer the strengths portion of the question without any hesitation. Since you are forced to pick a weak area, you must choose the one least used in your occupation. For most IT project management jobs, it would be Procurement Management. In any case, you must say that it is a weakness because you have not had formal training, or as much training in it. Training is something that can be quickly corrected.

> "My strengths are in the areas of Scope and Time management.
> A weakness I have is in the Procurement Management area, as I have
> not had formal training in it."

3.47 What are the risks you had in your last project?

Risk is a hot topic today, and if you put in your resume that you managed risk, you must have actual examples to speak of.

> "There were two team members that were new at the roles they
> had been assigned, and that could delay the project. I took steps to
> mitigate the risk, but their inexperience ended up delaying the project.

> Another risk we had was that the software we were to use had not
> really been tested in production and could have problems that could
> delay our project."

3.48 What is the role of Information Technology in a company?

"The role of Information Technology is to support the business"

3.49 Name three signs that indicate your project may fail.

They are poorly defined scope, loss of executive sponsorship and continuous change in business needs.

3.50 More questions

- What would be the ideal job environment for you as a project manager?
- What are the areas of Project Management Knowledge?
- What areas of the Project Management Body of Knowledge do you think are your weakest?
- What is the role of information technology in your current job?
- What would your boss say about you?
- What are your career goals? How do you see this job affecting your goals?

- Tell me about a situation where your loyalty was challenged. What did you do? Why?
- In what types of situations is it best to abandon loyalty to your manager?
- Describe what you think it would be like to do this job every day.
- What do you believe qualifies you for this position?
- What have you learned from your failures?
- Of your previous jobs, which one did you enjoy the most? What did you like the most/least? Why? What was your major accomplishment? What was your biggest frustration?
- Tell me about special projects or training you have had that would be relevant to this job.
- What are some things that you would not like your job to include?
- What are your current work plans? Why are you thinking about leaving your present job?
- Describe an ideal job for you.
- If I were to contact your former employer, what would he/she say about your decision-making abilities?
- Give me an example of a win-win situation you have negotiated.
- Tell me about your verbal and written communication ability. How well do you represent yourself to others? What makes you think so?
- Give me an example of a stressful situation you have been in. How well did you handle it? If you had to do it over again, would you do it differently?
- How do you deal with stress, pressure and unreasonable demands?
- Tell me about a tough decision you had to make.
- Describe what you did at your workplace yesterday.
- How would you solve the following technical problem?
- What strengths did you bring to your last position?
- Describe how those contributions impacted results.
- What are the necessary steps to successful project management?
- How do you plan for a project?
- What is important to consider when planning a *(your type of)* project?
- What are things that you have found to be low priority when planning for *(your type of project)?*
- What distinguishes a project from routine operations?
- What are the three constraints on a project?
- What are the five control components of a project?
- What experience have you had in project management?
- Tell us about a project in which you participated and your role in that project.
- When you are assigned a project, what steps do you take to complete it?
- As you begin your assignment as a project manager, you quickly realize that the corporate sponsor for the project no longer supports it. What will you do?
- Tell us about a successful project in which you participated and how you contributed to the success of that project.

- Your project is beginning to exceed budget and fall behind schedule due to almost daily user change orders and increasing conflicts in user requirements. How will you address the user issues?
- You've encountered a delay in an early phase of your project. What actions can you take to counter the delay? Which actions will have the most effect on the result?
- How do you plan a project?
- What is a Gantt chart?
- What is a critical path?
- What is a project charter?
- What is WBS?
- What is earned value?
- What is a "project milestone"?
- What is "project float"?
- Explain the key differences between project and program management.
- What actions are required for successful executive sponsorship of a project?
- Describe a situation in which you were able to use persuasion to successfully convince someone to see things your way.
- Describe a time when you were faced with a stressful situation that demonstrated your coping skills.
- Give me a specific example of a time when you used good judgment and logic in solving a problem.
- Give me an example of a time when you set a goal and were able to meet or achieve it.
- Tell me about a time when you had to use your presentation skills to influence someone's opinion.
- Give me a specific example of a time when you had to conform to a policy with which you did not agree.
- Please discuss an important written document you were required to complete.
- Tell me about a time when you had to go above and beyond the call of duty in order to get a job done.
- Tell me about a time when you had too many things to do and you were required to prioritize your tasks.
- Give me an example of a time when you had to make a split-second decision.
- What is your typical way of dealing with conflict? Give me an example.
- Tell me about a time you were able to successfully deal with another person even when that individual may not have personally liked you (or vice versa).
- Tell me about a difficult decision you've made in the last year.
- Give me an example of a time when there was something you tried to accomplish and failed.
- Give me an example of when you showed initiative and took the lead.
- Tell me about a recent situation in which you had to deal with a very upset customer or co-worker.

- Give me an example of a time when you motivated others.
- Tell me about a time when you delegated a project effectively.
- Give me an example of a time when you used your fact-finding skills to solve a problem.
- Tell me about a time when you missed an obvious solution to a problem.
- Describe a time when you anticipated potential problems and developed preventive measures.
- Tell me about a time when you were forced to make an unpopular decision.
- Please tell me about a time you had to fire a friend.
- Describe a time when you set your sights too high (or too low).
- What was the most complex project that you ever managed? What made it complex?
- What was the toughest phase of the *XYZ* project that you managed?
- What kept you awake at night in your most recent project?
- What percent of your projects missed planned schedules?
- If you were to do one thing differently in your most recent project, what would that be?
- What happened when you missed the schedule for *XYZ* project?
- Explain a situation that caused a major team conflict. What caused it?
- What mistakes do you think you made that started a conflict in the team? What would you do differently in future?
- Explain a project where the customer wanted new features added to the product.
- What happened when the management was unhappy with the project's progress? How did you handle the situation?
- Explain a situation where there was a problem team member.
- Exactly what steps did you take in *XYZ* project to build team spirit and morale?
- In the *ABC* program that you managed, how did you come up with the cost estimate? Did you do all the estimation yourself?
- How accurate was your estimate? Why was there a discrepancy?
- If you were to run your *ABC* project with a very lightweight project management process, what would be the three most important things that you would do?
- Give an example of change control that you used in your *XYZ* project.
- How did you ensure that scope was correctly captured in your projects or programs?
- In your *XYZ* program, how did you ensure that cross-functional teams worked in cohesion?
- Did you carry out scenario analysis of your projects?
- Regarding the *XYZ* project that you carried out at your *"Past Company Inc"*, if you were to manage a similar project for our company's website, how would you go about doing it? (.)

- Our online product configuration project is running late and over budget by $1 million. You are hired to replace the previous project manager. What would be the things you would do on your first day and first week once you arrive on board?
- What is your project about? What stage or phase is it currently in? What is your current role in your project?
- Explain how you manage requirements in your project.
- Where and how do you document your requirements?
- What and where are the policy statements for requirement management?
- How do you ensure that you base your software plans, work items and products on the requirements?
- If at some stage in the life cycle the initial requirements change, what will you do? How will you handle any changes in the requirements?
- Explain the contract review process followed in your project.
- When requirements change, how do you handle the changes it may lead to in the project progress and schedule?
- How do you handle any risk that might arise due to changes in requirements?
- How do you ensure that you are consistently meeting the requirements during various stages in the life cycle of the software product?
- How do internal quality audits cover requirements management activities in the project?
- Who is responsible for managing the requirements in your project?
- What will you do if you find that you cannot meet the requirements?
- What training have you undergone in project planning?
- How do you ensure that your project plan is available for others to see? Where will you find the plans of other projects executed (in the past or currently) in the center?
- How did you choose the appropriate life cycle for your project?
- What are the documents that you will refer to in order to create the plan?
- How do you estimate the effort for your project? Where is the estimation procedure documented?
- What procedures do you follow to arrive at the project schedule?
- Where and how are the risks associated with your project identified and documented?
- When you come into the office, how do you know what you have to do during the day?
- How do you report the status of your project?
- How are the team members kept informed about the current status of the project?
- How do the audits cover planning activities?
- How does the senior management review your project's progress?
- How do you track the technical activities in your project?
- How is the status of the project communicated to the team?

- How do you track the size or changes in size of the work products in your project?
- When do you revise your project plan? When do you know you have to revise your project plan? Where is the plan revision frequency documented?
- How do you ensure that you and all the other team members on your project have the required technical skills to execute the project?
- How do you assign tasks to your team members?
- What is the document that should be consulted to know about your project, the activities you do, your schedules and milestones?
- What and where are the policy statements that dictate quality assurance in your project?
- How are the quality assurance activities planned?
- In *Project QA*, what would a non-conformance report be?
- Do you have experience with project audits?
- What would an internal quality audit involve? What would happen during this audit?

Section 4   Job Interviewer Guide

To win the battle you must know your adversary. While the job interviewer might not really be your adversary, you still need to know how he/she operates.

How to Interview (The interviewer view)

When interviewing a candidate for a job there are three things that you must answer at the end of the interview:

1. Can the candidate do the job? Does he have the skills to do it?
2. Would the candidate do the job? Is he going to be motivated and would he stay challenged? Would he be able to commute, move, etc?
3. Would the candidate fit in the company culture?

When the screening of the candidates is done, you will bring the top two or three in for an interview. What questions should you ask them? What answers should you be looking for? How will you know which one to hire? Whether you work for a large company with a human resources department and volumes of procedures, or you're a small business owner with a few employees, the questions you want to ask are the same. They are questions that tell you, in increasing order of importance:

1. Whether the person has the skills to do the job
2. How they function under pressure

3. How well they will fit into the team

Can They Do the Job?

This is perhaps the easiest question. You have seen the person's resume so you know they claim to have the necessary skills.

Ask a few questions to verify what they claim.

- "I see you managed the payroll for three subsidiaries. What was the most difficult part of integrating all of them?"
- "When you were the marketing manager for *ABC company,* what were the steps you took when planning the annual marketing budget?"
- "I see you program in *(whatever language).* How do you do a loop?

Notice these questions ask how or what. They cannot be answered yes or no. Listen to the answer to see how quickly they answer, how complete/correct their answer is, and whether they actually answer what you asked or go off onto something with which they are more familiar.

How Well Do They Function Under Pressure?

This may be the area where most managers have trouble asking good questions, but they are more important than the job competency questions above. We are reluctant to be the "bad guy" and put someone under pressure. However, there are very few jobs, and certainly none that report to you, that don't place the employee under stress from time to time. Anybody can do well in calm times. You want people who can function well when things get confusing or difficult. To identify which candidate will perform best under pressure, you must ask tough, stressful questions.

- "What makes you think you are better for this job than all the other candidates?"
- "Tell me about a stressful situation that occurred repeatedly on your last job and how you handled it."
- "Which co-worker at your last job did you get along with least well? What did you do about it?"

Again, the important thing is how quickly, directly and completely they answer your questions. If a candidate says he has never been under stress, avoid that person. Either he is lying or he is out of touch with reality. If a candidate says she gets along with all her co-workers and never has a conflict with anyone, press for more information. She is either a saint or a doormat.

One question I like to ask here is, "What did you think of our website?" It tells me whether the person has taken the time to visit our website to learn about the company, but it also tells me how they will respond to the pressure of being put on the spot.

How Well Will They Fit In?

Among equally qualified candidates, this is the most important attribute. You need someone who will fit in with the team and be a productive member, and someone who will add to the team and not be a distraction. Be careful, though. You aren't looking for the "nicest" person. You are looking for the best fit. In addition to personality, you need to evaluate work habits, a complementary skill set and where the team needs help.

In a very low-key office, a loud, boisterous new hire would probably decrease the team's production because the team would be busy wondering why the person is so loud. On the other hand, someone moderately outspoken could be just what the team needs to get them fired up and producing again at top levels.

Similarly, If everyone in the group comes in between 8:30 and 9:00 but works until 6:00 PM or later, it will be difficult for a new hire to fit in if he/she always come in at 6:30 or 7:00 so he/she can leave at 3:00 PM.

When you interview candidates for a job opening, you need to ask questions to be sure they can do the job, but it is even more important to ask questions to make sure they can handle stress and that they will fit in with the team.

This space intentionally left blank

Part 2 - Project Management Theory

Section 1   Project Management in One Page (or Three)

Managing a project can be daunting. Whether planning a bridge, developing a new website or building a business, you need to employ project management techniques to help you succeed. I'll summarize the top seven best practices at the heart of good project management in order to help you to achieve project success.

Define the Scope and Objectives

First, understand the project objectives. Suppose your boss asks you to organize a golf tournament. Is the objective to get as much entry fees as possible, or is it to do some bonding exercise? Deciding the real objectives will help you plan the project.

Scope defines the boundary of the project. Is the organization of transportation to take staff to the golf tournament within scope, or should staff make their own way there? Deciding what's in or out of scope will determine the amount of work that needs performing.

Understand who the stakeholders are, what they expect to be delivered and get their support. Once you've defined the scope and objectives, make sure the stakeholders review and agree with them.

Define the Deliverables

You must define what will be delivered by the project. If your project is a new purchasing system, then one deliverable might be the training. So, decide what tangible items will be delivered and document them. You need to make clear to the sponsors of the project what it is that they will have once the project is completed

Sponsors and Key stakeholders must review the definition of deliverables and must agree they accurately reflect what must be delivered.

Project Planning

Planning requires that the project manager decides which people, resources and budget are required to complete the project.

You must define what activities are required to produce the deliverables using techniques such as Work Breakdown Structures. You must estimate the time and effort required for each activity, dependencies between activities and a realistic schedule to complete them. Involve the project team in estimating how long activities will take. Set milestones which indicate critical dates during the project. Write this into the project plan. Get the key stakeholders to review and agree to the plan.

Communication

Project plans are useless unless they've been communicated effectively to the project team. Every team member must know their responsibilities. In the same vein, the status of the project must be communicated to all stakeholders and surprises should be avoided. A communication plan specifying what communications will take place, the frequency of those communications and the participants must be created.

Tracking and Reporting Project Progress

Once your project is underway, you must monitor and compare the actual progress with the planned progress. You will need progress reports from project team members. You should record variations between the actual and planned cost, schedule and scope. You should report variations to your manager and key stakeholders and take corrective actions if variations get too large.

You can adjust the plan in many ways to get the project back on track, but you will always end up juggling cost, scope and schedule. If the project manager changes one of these, then one or both of the other elements will inevitably need changing. It is juggling these three elements - known as the project triangle - that typically causes a project manager the most headaches!

Change Management

Stakeholders often change their mind about what must be delivered or the business environment changes after the project starts, so assumptions made at the beginning of the project may no longer be valid. This often means the scope or deliverables of the project will change. If a project manager accepted all changes into the project, the project would inevitably go over budget, be late or might never be completed.

By managing changes, the project manager can make decisions about whether to incorporate the changes immediately or in the future, or to reject them. This increases the chances of project success because the project manager controls how the changes are incorporated, can allocate resources accordingly and can plan when and how the changes are made. Not managing changes effectively is often a reason why projects fail.

Risk Management

Risks are events that can adversely affect the successful outcome of the project. I've worked on projects where risks have included staff lacking the technical skills to perform the work, hardware not being delivered on time, lack of integration and many others. Risks will vary for each project, but the main risks to a project must be identified as soon as possible. Plans must be made to avoid the risk or, if the risk cannot be avoided, to mitigate the risk to lessen its impact if it occurs. This is known as risk management.

You don't manage all risks because there could be too many, and not all risks have the same impact. So identify all risks, estimate the likelihood of each risk occurring, estimate its impact on the project and then multiply the two numbers together to give the risk factor. High risk factors indicate the severest risks. Manage the ten with the highest risk factors. Constantly review risks and look out for new ones since they have a habit of occurring at any moment.

This space intentionally left blank

Section 2   Project Management and Its Context

A <u>project</u> is a temporary endeavor undertaken to create a unique product or service. It has a definite starting and ending point.

A <u>program</u> is a group of related projects managed in a coordinated way and is ongoing.

2.1   Project Management

The challenge of project management is to ensure that a project is delivered within the defined constraints. The second, more ambitious challenge is the optimized allocation and integration of the inputs needed to meet those pre-defined objectives. The project, therefore, is a carefully selected set of activities chosen to use resources (time, money, people, materials, energy, space, provisions, communication, quality, risk, etc.) to meet the pre-defined objectives.

Project management is a combination of disciplines. For example, the project management of software projects has the following components:

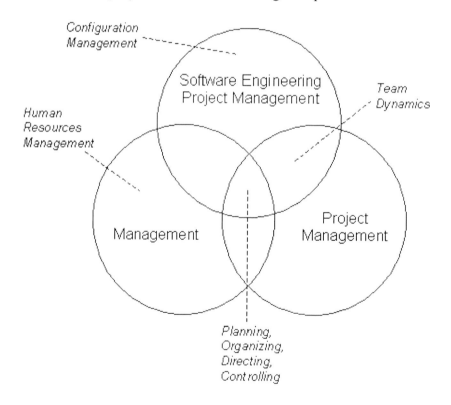

2.2   The Traditional Triple Constraint

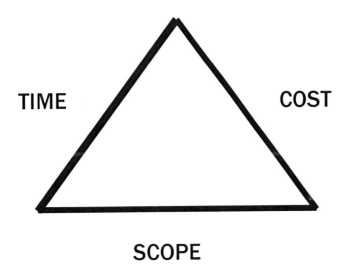

Time	Cost	Scope
Time required for completing all tasks contributing to the completion of each component	Cost to develop a project depends on several variables including (chiefly), labor rates, material rates, equipment, management and profit	Requirements specified for the end result

Like any human undertaking, projects need to be performed and delivered under certain constraints. Traditionally, these constraints have been listed as scope, time and cost. A further refinement separates product 'quality' or 'performance' from scope and turns quality into a fourth constraint.

The time constraint refers to the amount of time available to complete a project. The cost constraint refers to the budgeted amount available for the project. The scope constraint refers to what must be done to deliver the project. These three constraints compete with each other.   Increased scope typically means increased time and increased cost. A tight time constraint could mean increased costs and reduced scope, and a tight budget could mean increased time and reduced cost.

The discipline of project management is about providing the tools and techniques that enable the project team (not just the project manager) to organize their work to meet these constraints.

2.3 Project Stakeholders

Project stakeholders are individuals and organizations that are actively involved in the project, or whose interests may be positively or negatively affected by the result of project execution.

- Project manager
- Customer/user
- Performing organization
- Project team member
- Sponsor

2.4 Attributes of a Project Manager

Attributes expected from a project manager
- Leadership
- Communication and coordinating skills
- Attention to detail
- Problem solving skills
- Decision making skills
- Negotiating skills
- Facilitating skills
- Capable of understanding individuals
- Able to cope with ambiguity, setbacks and disappointments
- Ability to view the organization's goals
- Results-oriented
- Can-do attitude
- Politically savvy
- Ability to influence others

While organizations tend to promote the technical experts to project leadership positions, being a technical expert does not have to be an attribute of a project manager.

2.5 Project Life Cycle

Projects will usually be divided into *Project Phases*. The project phases are known as the *Project Life Cycle*.

At the conclusion of each project phase, a review of project performance to date is done to determine if the project should continue into its next phase, and to detect and correct errors.

The project life cycle serves to define the beginning and the end of a project, and it can be used to link the project to the ongoing operations of the performing organization. It defines:

- What work should be done in each phase
- Who should be involved in each phase

Project life cycle characteristics:

- Cost and staffing levels are low at the start, higher toward the end and drop rapidly as the project draws to a conclusion.
- The probability of successfully completing the project is lowest, and hence risk and uncertainty are highest, at the start of the project. The probability of successful completion gets progressively higher as the project continues.
- The ability of a stakeholder to influence the final characteristics of the project's product and the final cost of the project is highest at the start and gets progressively lower as the project continues.
- A key deliverable is completed at the end of each phase..A deliverable is a tangible and verifiable work product.

The project life cycle often consists in three phases:

1. Definition
2. Construction
3. Closure

Typical Life Cycle

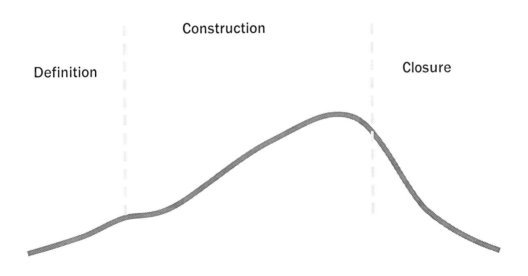

Construction

Definition

Closure

2.6 Project Phases

This section discusses the major phases of a project in a chronological order. The tools and work products mentioned will be described in the following section, Project Management Areas of Knowledge.

Project Initiation

Projects are selected from competing projects based on diverse factors that include cost/benefits analysis and politics.

Project Selection is the process of analyzing the project's potential benefits and its estimated costs to determine if it should be executed.

Project initiation is the most important step in the formal definition and authorization of a project. In most organizations, it starts with a project charter, but other organizations create the project charter after some planning has been done.

At minimum, the project initiation should generate a project definition document that identifies the objectives and requirements of the project, the stakeholders, the timeline and the resources to be used.

The objectives and requirements of the project as defined in the initiation will be the input for the project planning phase.

Project Planning

- Project planning consists of creating a consistent, coherent and comprehensive document that formalizes and details the work to be done.
- It is a guide to project execution and project control.
- Specifies the line of command and the line of communications among the different stakeholders.
- The most important tool for project planning is the Work Breakdown Structure (WBS). It breaks the project into a product- or task-oriented diagram.
- Projects are exposed to risks, and those risks should be considered while doing project planning.
- Projects can be estimated in a top-down or bottom-up approach. Top-down approach is acceptable in the early stages of planning.
- Network diagrams should be used to identify the relationships between tasks.
- The critical path method is the most important tool used for estimating timelines.
- Fast tracking and crashing could be considered to speed up the schedule even though they increase the project risk.

- Human resources actually execute the project, and careful consideration should be given to resource use and availability.
- Resource leveling should be used to balance resources and use them more effectively throughout the life of the project, even though that may delay the timeline.

Project Execution and Project Control

- Project execution consists of completing the tasks specified on the project schedule following the procedures specified in the project plan.
- The project manager must assemble the team and manage each individual from the technical and human dimensions points of view.
- During the execution of the project, the project manager's role is to motivate the team members and keep them on focus.
- Project managers will use situational management to keep the team progressing towards completion.
- Project control consists of monitoring the project to determine if and how it is following the project plan.
- The key tool of project control is change management. Change management is a formal process for identifying change requests, putting them through a decision process and implementing the decision.
- Project progress should be reported frequently, and the use of techniques like earned value should be considered to measure project control.
- Fast tracking and crashing should be considered to remedy delays.

Project Closing

- Project termination is a process that must not be overlooked and consist of bringing a project to conclusion in an orderly fashion.
- At project closeout, the project should be evaluated and lessons learned should be communicated to the organization.
- Team must be dismissed in an orderly fashion.
- Even if a project is canceled before completion, the project must be closed properly.
- The project closing documentation of one project may be the input for another project.

2.7   Projects and organizations

The way a project is organized within an organization influences its operation. The organization's influence depends on the following:

- Organizational Systems
  - Project-based organizations
  - Process-based organizations
- Organizational Cultures
  - Shared values, norms, beliefs, expectations
  - Policies, procedures
  - Authority relationships
- Organizational Structure
  - Organizational structure constraints, the availability of and the terms under which resources become available to the project

This space intentionally left blank

2.8   Functional Organization

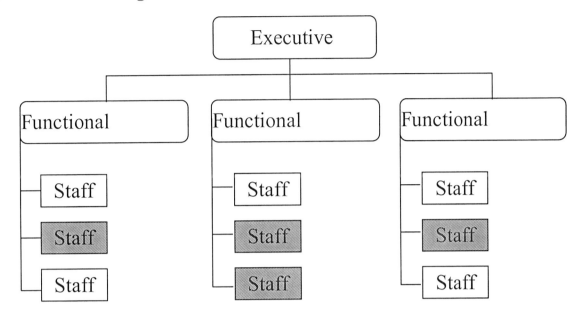

(Shaded Boxes represent staff engaged in project)

- A functional manager takes project management leadership
- Each employee has one clear superior
- Staff members are grouped by specialty
- Strong specialist competence is developed
- The perceived scope of the project is limited by the boundaries of the organization
- Lack of integration among different functions involved in the project
- Project manager has no formal authority for resources and must rely on informal power structure and his own interpersonal skills to obtain resource commitments from functional managers

This space intentionally left blank

2.9 Projectized Organization

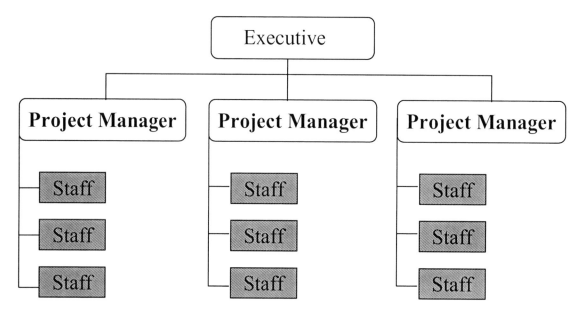

(Shaded Boxes represent staff engaged in project activities)

- Strongly project-oriented
- Reactivity against changes
- Better integration among different competencies
- Less efficiency in utilizing resources
- A separate, vertical structure is established for each project. All the project team members report directly and solely to the project manager.

2.10 Matrix Organization

- Trade-off between project objectives and business goals
- Coordination is attained through a functional organization
- Difficulty in managing conflicts in decision-making
- Balance of power leans towards the project manager

This space intentionally left blank

Weak Matrix Organization

(Shaded Boxes represent staff engaged in project activities)

- The project manager is a member of the staff
- Vertical functional lines of authority maintained with a relatively permanent horizontal structure containing managers for various projects
- Balance of power leaning toward the functional manager can cause a project to fall behind, because functional managers are pulling resources away to perform non-project-related tasks
- Under this model, the project manager may be able to make resource decisions on his own but not technical decisions

This space intentionally left blank

Balanced Matrix Organization

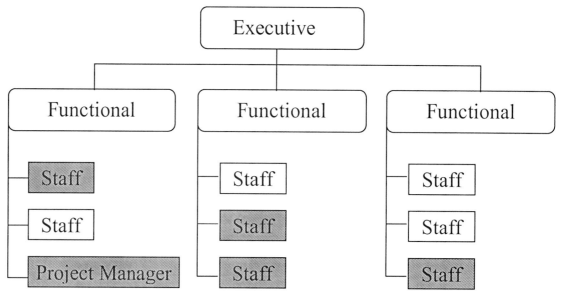

(Shaded Boxes represent staff engaged in project activities)

In the balanced matrix organization, there are project manager professionals as members of the staff.

Strong Matrix Organization

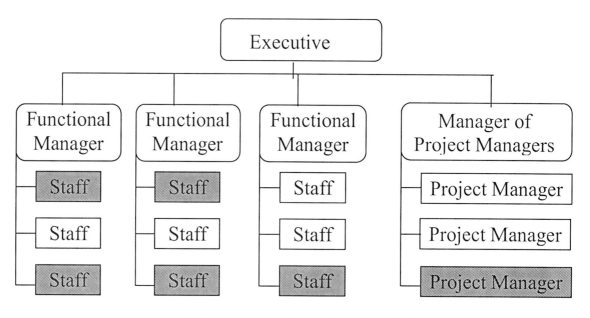

(Shaded Boxes represent staff engaged in project activities)

In the strong matrix organization, there is an organization formed by project managers.

2.11 Project Management Office

The Project Management Office (PMO) in a business or professional enterprise is the department or group that defines and maintains the standards of process generally related to project management within the organization. The PMO strives to standardize and introduce economies of repetition in the execution of projects. The PMO is the source of documentation, guidance and metrics in the practice of project management and execution.

This space intentionally left blank

Section 3 Project Management Areas of Knowledge

Process Groups / Knowledge Area	Initiating	Planning	Executing	Controlling	Closing
Project Integration Management		• Project Plan development	• Project Plan execution	• Integrated change control	
Project Scope Management	• Initiating	• Scope planning • Scope definition		• Verification • Change control	
Project Time Management		• Activity definition • Activity sequencing • Duration estimating • Schedule development		• Schedule control	
Project Cost Management		• Resource planning • Cost estimating • Cost budgeting		• Cost control	
Project Quality Management		• Quality planning	• Quality assurance	• Quality control	
Project H. R. Management		• Organizational planning • Staff acquisition	• Team development		
Project Communication Management		• Communication planning	• Information distribution	• Performance reporting	• Adm. Closure
Project Risk Management		• Risk planning • Risk identification • Qualitative and Quantitative risk analysis • Risk response planning		• Risk monitoring and control	
Project Procurement Management		• Procurement planning • Solicitation planning	• Solicitation • Source selection • Contract administration		• Contract closeout

Section 4 Project Integration Management

Project integration management is the area of knowledge of project management that covers the processes required to ensure that the various elements of the project are coordinated.

There are three main areas under project integration management:

1. Project plan development
2. Project plan execution
3. Change control

4.1 Project Plan Development

- Project plan development consists of creating a consistent, coherent and comprehensive document that formalizes and details the work to be done.
- It is a guide for project execution and project control.
- Specifies the line of command and the communications among the different stakeholders.

Project planning includes *project scheduling* but they should not be confused.

Components of a project plan:

- Project charter
- Project management approach or strategy
- Scope statement
- Performance measurement baselines
- Major milestones
- Staff
- Risks
- Scope and change management plans
- Risk management plan
- Communications plan
- Quality assurance plan
- Organization structure
- Cost estimates and scheduled dates

4.2   Project Plan Execution

Project plan execution is the process of executing the project plan and performing the tasks specified on it.

4.3   Change Control

Most of change management has to do with scope management, and it is described under Project Scope management.

Section 5 Project Scope Management

Scope management is the process that ensures that the project includes all the work required and only the work required to complete the project successfully.

The following processes are part of project scope management:

- Scope initiation
- Scope definition
- Scope planning
- Scope change control
- Scope verification

5.1   Scope Initiation

Scope initiation is the process of authorizing a project or that an existing project can continue into its next phase.

Portfolio Project Management

Before projects can be executed they must be selected from among other projects in the organization.

Project Selection – Two basic approaches

- Cost/benefit analysis
- Scoring or ranking models

Cost/Benefit Analysis

- Traditional approach that attempts to quantify the costs and savings (or revenue) associated with potential projects
- A variety of techniques can be used:
  - Net present value (NPV)
  - Payback period
  - Internal rate of return (IRR)
  - Return on investment (ROI)
- NPV is generally the preferred approach

Limitations of cost/benefit analysis

- Difficult to apply to certain projects
- Project may have intangible benefits
- Project may be strategic
- Failure to account for important qualitative or subjective factors may distort the project selection process
- Scoring and ranking models represent an attempt to correct this problem

Scoring and Ranking Models

- A variety of scoring and ranking models have been proposed
- Most models are based on a limited number of criteria deemed to be important in selecting projects
- Criteria generally include quantitative and qualitative factors
- Factors are frequently weighted to reflect their importance in the selection process
- Each project is evaluated against all the criteria and a single score is computed per project. The projects with the highest scores are given funding.

Limitations of scoring and ranking models

- Identifying an appropriate set of weights for the selection criteria can be a time-consuming process
- Output of these models is highly dependent on the weights that are assigned to different selection criteria
- The models force us to reduce a multidimensional set of criteria into a single number
- Like traditional cost/benefit analysis, these models focus on one project at a time

- Can use cost minimization or revenue maximization ranking

Project Definition Components

The project definition is sometimes called the *project charter* and will have the following elements:

- Summary definition of the project
- Objectives
- Background (programs, environment, history, related projects)
- Strategy
- Deliverables
- Timeline
- Assumptions
- Constraints
- Risks
- Resources
- Acceptance criteria
- Stakeholders

Project Charter

A project charter is a document that defines the project. It is used by upper management to mark the official creation of a project. The project charter must contain at minimum:

- The business need that the project is to address
- The product or desired results description
- Constraints and assumptions
- Timeline
- Budget or resource allocation
- Resources
- Risks

The charter provides the manager with the authority to dedicate resources to the project.

5.2   Scope Definition

Scope definition consists in progressively elaborating and documenting the project's product or outcome.

Scope planning consists in detailing the product and the boundaries of the product that will be created with the project.

Some potential components of the project may be eliminated at the beginning after some high level return on investment analysis.

Project requirements

Lack of proper requirements is the major cause of project failure.

Requirements definition guidelines:

- The best approach to define requirements is through feedback to the user of the understanding of the requirements. This can be done using graphic or physical means, prototyping, simulation, mock screens, etc.
- As important as describing what is included in the project is to mention what is not included in the project.
- Stress to the client that what is not in the requirements is not in the project.
- State all assumptions and constraints as part of the project definition.
- Project requirements must concentrate on the needs, not necessarily on the how.
- Establish a procedure to specify changes to the requirements.
- Joint Application Design and other new techniques should be considered

Work Breakdown Structure (WBS)

The WBS is a product-oriented division of the components of a project. It is used for defining and organizing the total scope of a project, using a hierarchical diagram.

While the best way to decompose a project is to describe the planned outcomes, a WBS is sometimes done decomposing the tasks.

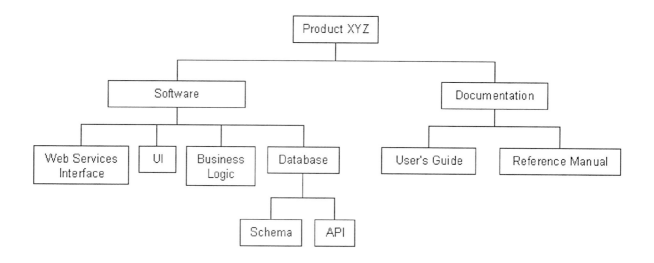

- The WBS is the foundation of project planning and control.
- The WBS must contain 100% of the project. If something is not in the WBS, it is not in the project.
- If the WBS is incomplete, the schedule and budget will be incomplete.
- *Work package* - the lowest level of the WBS. This is the level where work is assigned and progress is tracked.

5.3   Scope Change Control

Change is a reality in any project situation. Projects occur over a span of time, and time brings new circumstances and conditions. Projects are also completed by people, and people have new ideas, recognize mistakes and change their minds. Under these circumstances, it would be unwise, if not impossible, to proceed with any project without recognizing, accepting and preparing for the possibility of change. Also a large number of projects fail due to '*scope creep*'. Scope creep happens when apparently inconsequential additions to the scope are made. Each of these changes might not bring down a project, but some of them may bring unintended consequences, and their accumulation will drain resources and add time to the project. Lack of change control opens the door to scope creep.

To control the scope of your project, you need to undertake a strict change management process. This process ensures that changes to the project scope, deliverables, timescales or resources are formally defined, evaluated and approved prior to implementation.

The purpose of change control is to prevent downstream work from changing the direction of the project without proper verification and supervision. Change control assures that change is done following a pre-established process and that change does not derail the project.

Change management starts at the beginning of the project by establishing a change management plan. A change management plan establishes the process to make changes including who has the authority to make what kind of changes.

Change management should be applied not only to the final product of the project (scope) but also to each work product created during the project. Work product change management starts when a work product is reviewed and approved. At this stage it is said that the work product is *base-lined*. If during the course of subsequent work it is determined that the work product needs to be changed, it should be changed through a pre-established process of revision and re-approval.

The change control process includes:

- Revision
- Approval process
- Implementation
- Tracking
- Status reporting
- Closure

5.4   Scope Verification

Scope verification occurs at the end of the project to obtain the user's acceptance of the project. The user will verify that the product matches what was defined in the project plan and what was amended using change control.

Section 6   Project Time Management

Project time management consists of ensuring that the project will be completed in a timely manner.   The main processes are:

- Activity definition
- Activity sequencing
- Activity duration estimating
- Schedule development
- Schedule control

Activities are also called *tasks*.

Activity definition consists of documenting the work to be done and the outputs of each activity. In some cases, the description of the activity is clear if the project is following a known methodology. In other cases, the activity and the work product might have to be fully documented.

The most important tools the project schedule are network diagrams.

6.1   Network Diagrams

- Network diagrams illustrate the tasks and their relationships in time.
- The network diagram shows what precedent activities must be completed before any given activity can be started, and what following activities can be started when the activity is completed.
- The network diagram has arcs (or arrows) and nodes, with the arcs connecting the nodes.
- A network diagram can be created having the activities on the arcs or on the nodes. Today it is more popular to use activities on arcs.

Software like MS Project and Primavera use the concept of network diagrams to help define, sequence and schedule tasks.

6.2   Gantt Chart

A Gantt chart illustrates a project schedule showing the start and finish dates of the tasks of a project.

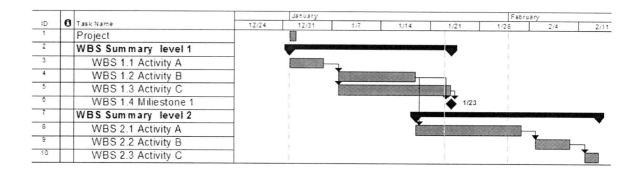

Milestones are markers that indicate important points in the timeline. They are represented in the Gantt chart, usually as diamonds, and represent the culmination or the start of a significant task or group of tasks.

6.3 Calculating the Project Duration

Some key concepts that help to understand schedule planning:

Working time refers to productive time needed to complete a project. It does not consider breaks, holidays or weekends, i.e. it takes 40 hours to write a given reporting program.

Elapsed time refers to chronological time and includes non-productive time such as lunchtime and breaks, i.e. the reporting.

Dependency refers to what is needed to start another task upon finishing one task. Dependencies could be more complex:

- Tasks could need to end together or start together
- A task would have to start for another to end

Leads and lags are elapsed time between tasks that share some dependency:

- Lag is time required between tasks, e.g. delay between ordering equipment and receiving it
- Lead (or negative lag): When the successor activity must start before the predecessor has completed

6.4 Critical Path Method

The Critical Path Method, also know as CPM, is a technique used to encounter the longest path in a network diagram between the beginning and the end of the project to identify the shortest time in which a project can be completed.

The essential method for using CPM is to construct a network diagram of the project that includes the following:

1. All activities required to complete the project
2. The time (duration) that each activity will take to completion
3. The dependencies between the activities

With these values, the CPM methodology calculates the starting and ending times for each activity, determines which activities are critical to the completion of a project (called the critical path), and reveals those activities with "float time" (those that can slide). The critical path is the sequence of project network activities with the longest overall duration, determining the shortest time possible to complete the project. Any delay of an activity on the critical path directly impacts the planned project completion date (i.e. there is no float on the critical path). A project can have several parallel critical paths. An additional parallel path through the network with the total durations shorter than the critical path is called a sub-critical or non-critical path.

There are two ways to reduce overall elapsed time in a project:

- *Crashing:* cost and schedule tradeoffs are analyzed to obtain the greatest amount of compression for the least incremental cost
- *Fast Tracking:* doing activities in parallel that would normally be done in sequence

6.5   PERT – Program Evaluation and Review Technique

- Another technique for doing schedule planning
- Uses a network diagram
- Used for tasks that have not been done before, for which estimates cannot be done with a reasonable level of exactitude
- Uses the following formula to calculate estimated task duration:

PERT Estimated time =

$$\frac{(Optimistic\ estimate)\ +\ 4\ \ X\ \ (Most\ likely\ estimate)\ +\ (Pessimistic\ estimate)}{6}$$

6.6   Project Schedule Control

Schedule control consists of ensuring that the project is being executed as planned and that the tasks are completed according to the timeframes in which they were supposed to be completed.

Schedule control is concerned with:

- Influencing the factors which create schedule changes to ensure that changes are agreed upon
- Determining that a schedule has changed
- Managing the actual changes when they occur

Tools for schedule control:

- Variance Analysis
  - o Comparing target dates with the actual and forecast start and finish dates
  - o It allows evaluating the project-time performance
- Earned Value

6.7   Earned Value

Earned Value Analysis (EVA) in its various forms is a widely accepted method of performance measurement. It is used to estimate how a project is doing in terms of schedule and budget.

Earned value is a measure of the value of work performed so far. It uses original estimates and progress-to-date to show whether the actual costs incurred are on budget and whether the tasks are ahead of or behind the baseline plan.

It can answer the following questions in time and money:

- Where are we now?
- Where are we going?

Earned Value Analysis (EVA) involves calculating three key values for each activity:

1. Planned Value
2. Actual Cost
3. Earned Value

Planned Value (PV) is the portion of the approved cost estimate planned to be spent on an activity during a given period.

Actual Cost (AC) is the total cost incurred in accomplishing work on the activity during a given period.

Earned Value (EV) is the value of the work actually completed.

Examples:

Planned Value, week 1
- Task 1: 10 hours at $200 per hour = $2,000
- Task 2: 20 hours at $200 per hour = $4,000

Results at the end of week 1:

Task 1:
- Hours worked: 12 => Actual Cost > (12 X $200) = $2,400
- Status (percent complete): 100%   (Completed):
- Earned Value % complete X   (Total Planned Value)
- Earned Value = (100% X $2000)) = $2,000

Task 2:
- Hours worked: 5 => Actual Cost > (5 X $200) = $1,000
- Status (percent complete): 50%:
- Earned Value % complete X   (Total Planned Value)
- Earned Value = (50% of $4,000) = $2,000

Earned Value Performance Indicators

Cost Variance (CV) = EV – AC
A positive value is good, while a negative value indicates trouble

Cost Performance Index (CPI) = EV / AC
Cost is under control if 0.95 < CPI < 1.10   (Use as a guide, not as a hard rule.)

If the CPI is over 1, the project is progressing at a lower cost than planned.

Schedule Variance (SC) = EV – PV
A positive value is good, while a negative value indicates trouble

Schedule Performance Index (SPI) = EV / PV
Schedule is under control if 0.95 < SPI < 1.10 (Use as a guide, not as a hard rule.)

If the SPI is over 1 the project is progressing at a faster rate than planned.

Other calculations:

Estimate at Completion (EAC) is a forecast of most likely total project costs based on project performance and risk quantification.

It can be calculated in different ways:

EAC = Actual due dates + new estimate for all remaining work
- Used when past performance shows that the original   estimating assumptions were fundamentally flawed

EAC = Actual due dates + remaining budget

- Used when current variances are seen as typical and the project management team expectations are that similar variances will not occur in the future

EAC = Actual due dates + remaining budget modified by a performance factor (CPI)

- Used when current variances are seen as typical of future variances

Notes about terminology:

Planned value is also called Budgeted Cost of Work Scheduled (BCWS).
Actual cost is also called Actual Cost of Work Performed (ACWP).
Earned value is also called Budgeted Cost of Work Performed (BCWP).

Earned value must be calculated at the level of cost control and this might be higher than the level of task control.

Section 7 Project Cost Management

Project cost management consists of assuring that the project is completed within the approved budget and is primarily concerned with the cost of resources used in the project.

There are four principal processes pertaining to project cost management:

- Resource planning
- Cost estimating
- Cost budgeting
- Cost control

7.1   Resource Planning

Resource planning is determining the quality and quantity of resources (people, equipment, materials) which should be used and when they are needed to perform project activities.

- *Resource leveling* consists of planning the project to use the resources most effectively or planning the project using limited resources.

- Resource leveling could imply longer project duration but less cost and less risk.
- Resource planning cannot be done independently of cost estimating, as there will be tradeoffs to consider. Some tradeoffs will even impact the project schedule.
- Provide an estimation of the needed resource levels to complete project activities.

7.2   Cost Estimating

- Different costing alternatives must be considered and evaluated.
- The cost estimating process must consider whether the cost of additional design work will be offset by expected savings.
- Cost estimating considers two types of costs:
    o   Costs associated with carrying out project tasks, such as materials and direct labor costs
    o   Costs associated with administering the project

Cost Estimating Tools

Analogous Estimating

- Using the actual cost of a previous, similar project as the basis for estimating the cost of the current project
- It is used when there is a limited amount of detailed information about the project
- It is the tool used when doing expert judgment

Parametric Model

Using project characteristics in a mathematical model to predict project costs. The accuracy of this model is high when:

- The historical information used to implement the model was accurate
- Parameters used are readily quantifiable
- Scalability

Top-down Estimating

- Based on applying analogous or parametric models to the major components of the project to get a grand total.

Bottom-up Estimating

- Estimating the cost of individual activities, then summarizing the individual estimates to get a project total
- The cost and accuracy is driven by the size and complexity of the individual activity
- Requires a WBS at its lowest level

Cost estimating risks

- Missing project components (incomplete WBS)
- Incorrect guesses
- Top-down estimates tend to be lower than actual for missing components
- Bottom-up estimates are too costly to make
- Political pressure, low-balling

7.3 Cost Control

- Monitoring cost performance to detect and understand variances from plan
- Ensuring that all appropriate changes are recorded accurately in the cost baseline
- Preventing incorrect, inappropriate or unauthorized changes from being included in the cost baseline
- Informing appropriate stakeholders of authorized changes
- Acting to bring expected costs within acceptable limits
- Searching out the causes of both positive and negative variances

A key tool for cost control is earned value, which was described in Section 6, Project Time Management.

Section 8 Project Quality Management

The quality knowledge area focuses on the quality of the projects processed and results. The quality planning process focuses on identifying standards, while the quality assurance process focuses on project performance. The quality control process focuses on evaluating project results.

Quality is achieved through planning, directing and implementing the actions that are consistent with the concept of "do the right thing right the first time." A dedicated effort of setting standards for the work, understanding the customer's requirements and implementing the requirements in all documentation and actions is needed to infuse quality into projects.

There are two main types of quality management that take place in a project:

- Quality of the project management process
- Quality of the work products

8.1 Quality of the Project Management Process

Controlling the quality of the project management process includes the following:

- Verify that the project plan includes the tasks as per project standards
- Verify that the project plan includes the creation of documents as defined by project standards
- Verify that the documents and processes defined in the project plan are actually being executed
- Verify that the planned gates on the project are being performed and that the project actually meets the requirements to pass the gate before continuing

Key points:

- Quality must be planned and built into the project as opposed to inspecting for quality at the end of the project
- The most important element to keep the quality of a project is to follow a consistent methodology for project execution
- The management of quality should start with the project
- Quality not only refers to the quality of the programs created, but also to the technical design, the functional specifications, and even to the project charter
- Use quality to verify conformance to requirements and fitness of use
- Optimal quality is reached at the point where incremental revenue from improvement equals the incremental cost to secure it
- Control Charts: Graphic display to determine if process is in control

8.2 Quality Assurance

- Planned and systematic activities implemented within the quality system to provide confidence that the project will satisfy the quality standards
- It consists in applying what has been developed in the quality planning process
- Quality issues must be divided into external and internal quality

Quality assurance tools

Quality Audit

- A structured review of quality management activities
- The objective is to identify lessons learned that can improve organization performance
- Troubles are classified in order to allow future audit
- Audit can often be performed by a third party
- It may be scheduled or random

8.3   Six Sigma

Six Sigma is a business improvement methodology to systematically improve processes by eliminating errors. *Errors* are defined as units that are not members of the intended population. The objective of Six Sigma is to deliver high performance, reliability and value to the end customer.

Sigma (the Greek letter σ) is used to represent standard deviation (a measure of variation) of a population, and Six Sigma covers 99.99% of the population. The aim of Six Sigma is to assure that at least 99.99% of the products produced are defect free, specifically only 3.4 defective parts per million.

This space intentionally left blank

8.4 Quality management process

The quality management process:

> **Quality Planning** – The processes required to ensure that the project will satisfy the needs for which it was undertaken.

$\downarrow$

> **Quality Assurance** – Strategic view of quality during the execution of the project undertaken. Takes place over the lifetime of the project.

$\downarrow$

> **Quality Control** – Operational view of quality during the execution of the project. Takes place at specific times over the lifetime of the project.

8.5 Other Key Quality Concepts

Deming's 14 Points

W. Edwards Demings redefined quality in the 1950s, and while his studies were oriented toward industrial production, his observations are pertinent to management in general.

1. Create constancy of purpose toward improvement of product and service, with the aim to become competitive and to stay in business, and to provide jobs.
2. Adopt the new philosophy. We are in a new economic age. Western management must awaken to the challenge, must learn their responsibilities and take on leadership for change.
3. Cease dependence on inspection to achieve quality. Eliminate the need for inspection on a mass basis by building quality into the product in the first place.
4. End the practice of awarding business on the basis of price tag. Instead, minimize total cost.
5. Improve constantly and forever the system of production and service to improve quality and productivity, and thus constantly decrease costs.
6. Institute training on the job.

7.   Institute leadership. The aim of leadership should be to help people and machines and gadgets to do a better job. Leadership of management is in need of overhaul, as well as leadership of production workers.

8.   Drive out fear so that everyone may work effectively for the company.

9.   Break down barriers between departments. People in research, design, sales and production must work as a team to foresee problems of production and in use that may be encountered with the product or service.

10. Eliminate slogans, exhortations and targets for the work force asking for zero defects and new levels of productivity. These slogans only create adversarial relationships, as the bulk of the causes of low quality and low productivity belong to the system and thus lie beyond the power of the work force.

11. Eliminate work standards (quotas) on the factory floor. Substitute leadership. Eliminate management by objective. Eliminate management by numbers, numerical goals and substitute leadership.

12. Remove barriers that rob the hourly worker of his right to pride of workmanship. The responsibility of supervisors must be changed from sheer numbers to quality. Remove barriers that rob people in management and in engineering of their right to pride of workmanship. This means abolishment of the annual merit increase.

13. Institute a vigorous program of education and self-improvement.

14. Put everybody in the company to work to accomplish the transformation. The transformation is everyone's job.

Pareto Theory

80% of the quality problems are originated on 20% of the reasons.

Section 9 Project Human Resource Management

This area of knowledge focuses on the people who execute and are involved with the project.

9.1   Project Team Management

- Project failures are most often attributed to human failure
- The goal of the project manager is to get the job done
- The jobs gets done through the people who execute the project
- The project manager's biggest concern during execution should be team and people development

- The project manager must work on the following areas:

- Leadership, inspiration, morale
- Team building
- Team motivation

9.2 Motivation theories

McGregor's Theory X and Y

Theory X
- Workers are inherently self-centered, lazy and lack desire for progress
- Worker's most important goal is to obtain money for the work done.
- Managers must keep a close eye on employees, as they need to be pushed to work
- Top-down authority management works best

Theory Y
- Workers are willing and eager to accept responsibility and the work that comes with it
- Workers are motivated by things beyond money
- Management only needs to create the environment for workers to produce, and they will do their best for the organization

This space intentionally left blank

Maslow's Hierarchy of Needs

Maslow proposed that human beings have a hierarchy of needs. Humans must satisfy certain needs before they can satisfy others, and they can be represented by a pyramid with body (physiological) needs at the bottom.

Maslow's Hierarchy

Body (Physiological) Needs such as air, warmth, food, sleep, stimulation and activity. This need concerns biological balance and stable equilibrium (homeostasis). These needs can be very strong because if deprived over time, the person will die.

Security (Safety) Needs such as living in a safe area away from threats. This level is more likely to be found in children as they have a greater need to feel safe.

Social (Love and Belongingness) Needs such as the love of family and friends.

Ego (Self esteem) Needs such as healthy pride. Ego needs focus on our need for self-respect and respect from others.

Self Actualization (Fulfillment) Needs such as purpose, personal growth and realization of potentials. This is the point where people become fully functional, acting purely on their own volition and having a healthy personality.

9.3   Management Styles

Autocratic (directive, dictatorial) management style:

- Directive, top-down approach, does not request nor accept input from subordinates
- May be effective in short term projects where time is absolutely critical
- Could be used to direct non-specialized labor in large projects
- Morale can be affected when this style is used
- Could foster an arbitrary decision-making environment
- Decision-making could lose sight of all factors

Laissez-faire (let do) management style:

- May be effective with highly effective or highly creative individuals that need freedom to do their work
- Morale is high as individuals feel that they are not supervised
- May lead to chaos
- May be inefficient as direction can change multiple times
- Does not work in projects that require quick decision making

Democratic management style:

- Decisions are made with input from team
- Consensus can be reached
- Morale tends to be high as team members are able to influence decisions or at least feel that they are listened to
- Is effective in most project management situations
- Projects may stray from the goals of the organization

Autocratic–Paternalist management style:

Similar to autocratic, but the well-being for the subordinate is an important input to decision making.

Situational management style:

Situational management says that a project manager must use any of the management styles as the situation demands it.

Section 10 Project Communications Management

The project communications management area of knowledge focuses on communicating appropriate project information inside the project team and to all stakeholders. It provides a critical link between people, ideas and information at all stages in the project life cycle. Project managers should be spending about 60% to 80% of their time communicating. Formal processes aid in decision-making and help to achieve a successful project.

10.1 Communications Planning

Communications planning is the process of ascertaining the information and communication needs of project stakeholders. It creates the communications management plan.

The communications management plan:

- Is a document that guides project communications
- A description of a collection and filing structure for gathering and storing various types of information
- A distribution structure describing what information goes to whom, when and how
- A format for communicating key project information
- A project schedule for producing the information
- Access methods for obtaining the information
- A method for updating the communications management plans as the project progresses and develops

10.2   Information Distribution

Information distribution is the process of assuring the project stakeholders have the needed information available in a timely manner. Getting the right information to the right people at the right time and in a useful format is just as important as developing the information in the first place. Important considerations include:

- Using technology to enhance information distribution
- Formal and informal methods for distributing information

10.3 Performance Reporting

Performance reporting is the process of gathering and distributing project performance information including status reporting, progress measurement and forecasting. This process occurs within the Monitoring and Controlling Process Group.

- Performance reporting keeps stakeholders informed about how resources are being used to achieve project objectives
- Status reports describe where the project stands at a specific point in time
- Progress reports describe what the project team has accomplished during a certain period of time
- Project forecasting predicts future project status and progress based on past information and trends

- Status review meetings often include performance reporting

10.4 Administrative Closure

Administrative closure is generating, gathering and disseminating information to formalize phase or project completion. A project or phase of a project requires closure. Administrative closure produces:

- Project archives
- Formal acceptance
- Lessons learned

10.5 Suggestions for Improving Project Communications

- Manage conflicts effectively
- Develop better communication skills
- Run effective meetings
- Use e-mail effectively
- Use templates for project communications

10.6 Conflict Handling Modes

(in Preference Order)

- Confrontation or problem-solving: directly face a conflict
- Compromise: use a give-and-take approach
- Smoothing: de-emphasize areas of differences and emphasize areas of agreement
- Forcing: the win-lose approach
- Withdrawal: retreat or withdraw from an actual or potential disagreement

10.7 Running Effective Meetings

- Determine if a meeting can be avoided
- Define the purpose and intended outcome of the meeting
- Determine who should attend the meeting
- Provide an agenda to participants before the meeting
- Prepare handouts, visual aids, and make logistical arrangements ahead of time

- Run the meeting professionally
- Build relationships

Section 11 Project Risk Management

A <u>risk</u> is an uncertain event that, if it occurs, has a positive or negative effect on a project objective.

A <u>risk trigger</u> is an indication that a risk has occurred or is about to occur.

11.1 Risk Management

Risk management is the systematic process of identifying, analyzing and responding to project risk.

- Risk management minimizes the probability of adverse events and their consequences for project objectives.
- Risk management also looks to maximize the probability and consequences of positive events that may happen to the project.
- The risk management process must ensure that the level, type and visibility of risk management are commensurate with both the risk and importance of the project to the organization. (The same risk will have a different impact on different projects.)

This space intentionally left blank

11.2 Risk Management Process

The Risk Management Proces:

> **Risk Management Planning** – Decide how to approach and plan the risk management for the project.

↓

> **Risk Identification** – Determine which risks might affect the project and document their characteristics.

↓

> **Qualitative Risk Analysis** – Subjective analysis for occurrence, impact and criticality.

↓

> **Quantitative Risk Analysis** – Numerical analysis for occurrence, impact and criticality.

↓

> **Risk Response Planning** – Actions to take about identified risks.

↓

> **Risk Monitoring and Control** – Keep track of risks and plans, identify new risks and ensure execution of risk management and response plans.

Risk identification requires an understanding of the project's mission, scope and objectives of the owner and stakeholders. (Generic checklists may not cover all risks.)

11.3 Risk Management Plan

The risk management plan is how risk identification, qualitative and quantitative analysis, response planning, monitoring and control will be structured and performed during the project life cycle. It may include:

- Tools to be used
- Roles and Responsibilities: defines the lead, support, and risk management membership for each type of action in the risk management plan
- Reporting Formats: describes how the results of the risk management processes will be documented, analyzed and communicated to the project team, stakeholder and sponsor
- Tracking: documents how all facets of risk activities will be recorded for the benefit of the current project, future needs, and lessons learned

11.4   Risk Identification Tools

- Brainstorming
- Delphi Technique – The same questions are asked individually to different experts, to get an unbiased opinion
- Interviewing
- Strengths, Weaknesses, Opportunities and Threats (SWOT) Analysis
- External Risks
- Checklist created from similar projects

11.5   Qualitative Risk Analysis

Qualitative risk analysis is the process of assessing the impact and likelihood of identified risks. It prioritizes risks according to their potential effect on project objectives. The probability and consequences of the risks are evaluated using established qualitative–analysis methods and tools.

11.6   Quantitative Risk Analysis

Quantitative risk analysis looks to quantify the probability of each risk and its consequence on project objectives.

11.7 Risk Response Planning

Risk response planning is the process of developing options and determining actions to enhance opportunities and reduce threats to the project's objectives.

Mitigation:

Take steps to reduce the probability of the occurrence and the impact of the risk if it happens. It may take the form of implementing a new course of action that will reduce the problem (e.g. conducting engineering tests).

Avoidance:

Eliminate the risk by changing the project plan.

- It consists in changing the project plan to eliminate the risk or to protect the project objective from its impact.
- Obtaining information
- Improving communication
- Reducing scope to avoid high-risk activities
- Adding resources or time

Transference:

The risk is transferred to another entity. It will involve the payment of a risk premium and does not actually eliminate it, but transfers the ownership of it.

- It consists of seeking to shift the consequence of a risk to a third party.
- Transferring the risk gives another party the responsibility for its management. It doesn't eliminate it.
- It is most effective in dealing with financial risk exposure.
- It involves the payment of a risk premium to the party taking on the risk.

Acceptance:

If the response is acceptance, the team may develop a contingency plan so if the risk actually happens, there is a way to mitigate its impact. The impact could be so low (or so high) that no response is planned ahead of the occurrence.

11.8   Other Risk Definitions

Residual risks:

The risk that still exists when the primary risk has been mitigated, or transferred.

Secondary risk:

A risk that is generated when an action is taken to address an existing risk.

Risk Response Plan:

- Identified risks, their description, project areas affected, their causes
- Risk owners and assigned responsibilities
- Results from qualitative and quantitative risk analysis processes
- Agreed responses including avoidance, transference, mitigation, acceptance
- The residual risk
- Specific actions to implement the chosen response strategy
- Budget and time for response strategy
- Contingency plan and fallback plan

Risk Monitoring

- Keeping track of the identified risks, monitoring residual risks and identifying new risks
- Ensuring the execution of the risk plan
- Evaluating the risk plan's effectiveness in reducing risk
- It is an ongoing process for the life of the project

Section 12   Procurement Management

12.1   Requirements for a Contract

1. An offer
2. Acceptance
3. Consideration – something of value, not necessarily money
4. Legal capacity – separate legal parties, competent parties
5. Legal purpose – you cannot have a contract for illegal purposes

12.2   Solicitation Tools

Advertising

- Existing lists of potential sellers may often be expanded by placing advertisements in newspapers or in specialty publications

Bidder Conferences

- Meetings with prospective sellers prior to the preparation of proposals
- All prospective sellers must have a clear, common understanding of the procurement

Proposals

- Seller-prepared documents that describe seller's ability to provide the requested product
- Proposals may be supplemented with an oral presentation

Source Selection

- The receipt of bids or proposals and the application of the evaluation criteria to select a provider
- Price may be the primary determinant for an off-the-shelf item
- Proposals are separated into technical and commercial sections
- Multiple sources may be required for critical products

12.3   Contract Administration

- The process of ensuring that the seller's performance meets contract requirements
- Managing interfaces among the various providers
- The project management team must be aware of the legal implications of actions taken during a project

12.4 Contract Types

Lump Sum Contract or Fixed Bid

With this kind of contract, the contractor agrees to do a described and specified project for a fixed price. Fixed fee or lump sum contract is suitable if the scope and schedule of the project are sufficiently defined to allow the contractor to estimate project costs.

Time and Materials

Under this contract, the contractor gets paid an hourly rate and is paid for the expenses incurred. Used for consulting engagements.

Unit Price Contract

This kind of contract is based on estimated quantities of items included in the project and their unit prices. The final price of the project is dependent on the quantities needed to carry out the work.

In general, this contract is only suitable for construction and supplier projects where the different types of items, but not their numbers, can be accurately identified in the contract documents.

Cost Plus Contract

This is a contract agreement wherein the purchaser agrees to pay the cost of all labor and materials plus an amount for contractor overhead and profit (usually as a percentage of the labor and materials cost).

Incentive Contracts

Compensation is based on the contracting performance according to an agreed target - budget, schedule and/or quality.

About the Author

George T. Edwards obtained the Project Management Professional certification in 2003 and has over 20 years of project management leadership. Mr. Edwards has managed projects in the Americas and Europe for firms like Citibank, Toys "R" Us, Shell Oil, Kmart, Macy's and many other large corporations. Currently, he is the Information technology program manager for the expansion to Latin America of a US Fortune 50 company.

Mr. Edwards has worked for a Big 5 Management consulting firm, for global software companies and as an independent project management consultant. While most of his experience as a project manager has been in the information technology area, he also has experience with civil engineering projects.

Mr. Edwards holds degrees in Industrial Engineering, Information Systems and Computer Science.

LaVergne, TN USA
23 February 2010

174052LV00001B/14/A

9 780979 762338